Modernization: Latecomers and Survivors

Modernization: Latecomers and Survivors

MARION J. LEVY, JR.

Basic Books, Inc., Publishers

NEW YORK   LONDON

This book is affectionately dedicated to my father, who said to me when I was very young, "Son, I sure hope your idealism survives the day you realize that a large number of things in this world are determined by whose ox is gored," and to Beate Ruhm von Oppen, who is responsible for its being written but not for it.

Preface

There is not a single problem of moment in our world—either domestic or international—that is not involved with the process I refer to as modernization. I believe in strong statements, and this book contains a number of them. I hope they are sufficiently clear and baldly enough stated so that you can make up your mind about whether you agree or disagree with them. I have tried to avoid qualifications that might buy for them safety at the price of emptiness.

Personally, I do not care a great deal for modernization, although I am grossly habituated to her comforts. I have tried in this book to intrude my values as little as possible, but I do not wish to get involved in the tiresome argument about whether the statements I make are biased by my point of view. Of course they are. There is an explanation, in my motivation presumably, for every statement I make just as there is for every statement that anyone makes. Everyone has both general and particular biases—scientists (or pseudoscientists) are certainly no exception. Thus it may be that I write as I do because I am a fascist, a communist, a Jew, a racist, a sexist, a Galveston boy reared in comforting security, an elitist snob, or anything else you may wish to call me—I ask only that you keep in mind that whatever the explanation may be of *why* I write as I do, it does not follow that such an explanation either disproves or confirms what I have written.

I have a faith—that is the word for it—that it is possible to be scientific about human phenomena without any of the usual froth about the distinction between the "natural" sciences and the social (presumably unnatural?) sciences. Along with my faith, I have a special pretension. I fancy myself a theorist, a scientific theorist, no less. As such I owe you the warning that I hold myself to two major obligations. The first is to be intellectually honest, and the second is, to the best of my ability, to be interesting. I have not knowingly cut any corners on the former, and you will have to be the judge of the latter. I say this, however, to warn you further that as a scientist it is not my primary obligation to be *right*. Many readers will quite obviously and properly be more concerned with what is right, at least right in the sense of scientifically valid, about modernization, than with interesting hypotheses. After all, for many the solutions to very practical problems depend on their understanding of these phenomena. For those with policy responsibilities as well as the ordinary cares of life, it is terribly important to be right about these phenomena. Therefore, no matter how dogmatically I assert anything, the reader would be well advised as a matter of self-interest to regard everything I say as hypotheses about the facts and not as the facts themselves. I hope the discrepancies will not be great, but you should be on your guard.

None of the above should be construed as any sort of modesty—false or otherwise. In academia there are a few genuinely modest and humble scholars, but most of us have a choice between mock humble arrogance and forthright arrogance. I find the latter vastly the more amusing. I am every bit as arrogant as I appear to be.

I have tried to keep the scientific paraphernalia of this work to a minimum and to avoid technical terminology for which I have a penchant that amounts to a curse. Although definitions are near and dear to my heart, I have tried to use terms in close approximation to their ordinary usage. Definitions of the terms used and ad nauseum discussion of such scientific paraphernalia are to be found in a book of mine

Preface

entitled *Modernization and the Structure of Societies* (Princeton, N.J.: Princeton University Press, 1966). If I have been successful here, there will be little need for you to go there, but if you do, you will find more underpinning for what is here than you may wish.

Modernization is a very general problem, and I have tried to deal with that problem in a very general—very abstract—way. I believe that social scientists have been too little concerned with abstraction and too much involved with the detailed case. It is not that we have thought too much and felt too little; we have felt too much and hardly thought at all. Except for illustrations, every statement in this book is highly abstract. Some of the statements refer to generalities presumed to hold for all social life, whether that of the Trobriand Islander or the modern citizen of the Soviet Union. The other statements in the volume refer to uniformities that I believe to hold for any people who have been untouched by modernization, for any people who are latecomers to modernization, for any people who may be described as highly modernized, and for the processes of transition along that continuum.

It is one of the conceits of most people in highly modernized contexts that somehow what we do, if not proper and good, is at least normal, reasonable, and easily intelligible. The nonmodernized parts of human experience tend to be regarded as dubiously rational and above all as exotic and bizarre. Yet from all the evidence at our disposal, in terms of the total experience of humankind it is the patterns of the highly modernized that are the most exotic and the most bizarre, and—innate optimism to the contrary notwithstanding—we have yet to learn whether such patterns are even viable. Even if life may be sustained on this basis, many may question whether they will care to live so. We, the modernized, are the true queers of history.

Finally, although it is fashionable to treat racism as somehow of the essence of the problems of modernization, you will note that the subject of racism is not dealt with as a central issue in this volume. That is not an oversight; it is not callous indifference either. Unless the term "racism" is used as a synonym for human bigotry in general—as it so often is these days—racism, for all its disgusting, stupid, and cruel causes, characteristics, and effects, is one of the few of our great problems about which we have a cause to be optimistic, if only because of the recency of its development in the forms in which we know it today. For most of the world this specifically biologistically rationalized form of bigotry postdates, as an ignorant derivative, the scientific revolution of Charles Darwin in the second half of our nineteenth century. In our own country—and this is why U.S. slavery was the most awful form of slavery—this form of bigotry developed some decades precociously—in the early part of our nineteenth century—as a rationalization of the one set of people who both believed that all human beings were created free and equal and held slaves. That inconsistency remains our racism's greatest vulnerability. I think racism in this sense will be looked back upon as a shameful epiphenomenon. It is not central to the general structure of modernization for either firstcomers or latecomers. I believe it will pass, and I do not believe that either the past or the future of the matters discussed here would have been very different had human bigotry not hit on this variant when and as it did. This, of course, should in no way be taken as minimizing what this bigotry has cost its targets and its firers in cruel suffering, galling indignity, and base degradation.

I owe a debt to the graduate students of the Woodrow Wilson School who have helped me in many ways. That has been especially true in the case of Mr. Charles R. Bailey. Among my other colleagues I owe much to Professor Marvin Bressler for his patience and his ideas and to Professor Gilbert F. Rozman, who knows the materials I should know. Professors Norman Frohlich, Joe Oppenheimer, and Oran

Preface

Young tried to make me more abstract and logically complete. Professor Charles A. Berry preserved me from some of my primer errors in economics, and Professor Charles R. Frank's contribution is embedded as a dissent on pp. 73–74. Professor Clarence E. Ayres, to whom I owe a debt of more decades than either of us likes to recall, tried to preserve me from some of the same wrong-headedness he has warned me of so often before. Roger S. Pinkham of *Destructive Critics, Inc.* saw straight through me and what I wrote, as he always does. Professor David E. Apter helped me in ways that defy identification, as is his wont. But I also pressed this essay in draft on varied friends in varied walks besides scholastic ones. If the essay is readable, they repaid that pressure with a gift. Finally, this is not the first publication of mine for which Professor C. E. Black's help has been inestimable. The Center of International Studies and the Woodrow Wilson School of Princeton University have furnished a remarkably unrestrictive environment for work. I owe all of these and many others.

1972   Marion J. Levy, Jr.
                              *Woodrow Wilson School of Public
                                 and International Affairs
                              Princeton University*

Contents

PART I

*Introduction:
The Gist
of the Matter for
Latecomers*

Modernization as a Universal Social Solvent

The quest for origins has no end. This essay makes no pause for the beginnings of what we today call modernization.[1] I am only concerned with the nature of modernization,

[1] *Modernization*—I think that the ordinary use of this term will suffice, but if there are to be arguments about what the term means, I would take as the measure of modernization the ratio of inanimate to animate sources of power. The higher that ratio, the higher is the degree of modernization. There is, of course, no society totally lacking in some elements of both inanimate and animate sources of power, although the ratio may be very low indeed. There is also no society whose members make no use whatsoever of animate sources of power—no matter how highly modernized they become. As a minimum, however economical the process in power terms, decision-making involves the use of the brain, unless we reach the point at which all of our decisions are made by machines. I assume we shall never reach such a point. In this book, for ease of communication, I have used the terms "nonmodernized" and "modernized" or "highly modernized." Technically and properly the terms should be "relatively nonmodernized" and "relatively modernized," but those expressions are too cumbersome for present purposes. This book does not discuss the exact dividing line between nonmodernized (relatively nonmodernized) and modernized (relatively modernized) societies. It is concerned with cases well to one side or the other of this dividing line and the process of crossing it, though not with the actual point of crossing. I consider a society to be well on the modernized side of the line if the ratio of inanimate to animate sources of power is such that comparatively small decreases of that ratio would have far-reaching effects—effects almost certain to be judged by the people involved as catastrophic. More simply put, I regard a society as modernized whenever small decreases in uses of inanimate sources of power could not be made up by increases in animate sources of power without far-reaching social changes. Not the least of such changes might be radical increases in death rates. Modernization is defined here as the process of approaching that line, crossing that line, and/or moving further on the other side of that line. I regard that line as a point of no return or at least of no easy generally acceptable return, but that is not part of my definition. I have not tried to define the concept by what I regard as any of the most important features of modernization since I wish to make as little of the argument as possible true by definition.

the future of modernization, and the problems modernization poses for latecomers to the process. I do not think modernization to be as old as Eve. Indeed, I do not consider modernization to emerge full-figured at all until sometime into the nineteenth century. Most who have grown accustomed to her ways take them for granted and have lost all perspective on their extreme youth. As an "adult," modernization is no more than 150 years old by anyone's estimate, and most of the characteristics of modernization that we take for granted did not fully embrace the vast majority of even the firstcomers [2] until well into the twentieth century.

I do not treat the origins of modernization here because I do not know what they are, and I am not persuaded that any of my academic colleagues are very good on this subject either. Probably Max Weber remains more sophisticated on the origins of modernization than any other scholar. Increasingly, however, students have come to question either the tenability of his hypotheses or their relevance. Max Weber thought that the Protestant Ethic was a special (that is, the strategic necessary but not sufficient condition) factor that drove people over the edge into the development of what are here referred to as modernized societies. Even if he is correct, we simply regress to the question of what caused the Protestant Ethic at that time.

Still, modernization is interesting enough even if we leave the question of ancestry to heaven. Modernization is, after all, something new on the social scene—a kind of de-

---

[2] In what is to come I shall consistently distinguish between *firstcomers* and *latecomers* to modernization. *Firstcomers* refer to those people who, for whatever reasons, developed the patterns that we refer to as modernized ones when those patterns did not previously exist in the world. *Latecomers* refer to those who, whether by force of others or volition of their own or some combination of the two, took over or tried to take over some of these patterns from a developed model.

velopment of human patterns never seen before. Modernization is a universal social solvent.

The great social conquests, or cultural diffusions if one prefers, of the past have never had so broad and deep an impact on extremely general human lives and concerns. The greatest of the military conquests, probably those of Genghis Khan, wiped out many and changed more, but they left many almost entirely untouched; indeed, many of those taken, but not wiped out, persisted sufficiently unchanged to absorb the conquerors themselves. This latter was notably true of China, of course. In the nonmilitary realm, even the invention of printing and its possession for hundreds of years showed no comparable effects to those of modernization. The great religious diffusions can be dealt with in a comparably cavalier fashion.

Not so with modernization. Once developed—never mind how modernization grew or whence sprung—the following four propositions can be maintained: First, with the passage of time it becomes increasingly probable that the people possessed of these modernized patterns will come into contact with those who lack them. Second, once this contact is made—and quite regardless of whether force is used—it is increasingly probable that some of these modernized patterns will be taken up by those who have them not. Third, when those patterns are taken up, many of the indigenous (nonmodernized) patterns of the peoples concerned will come apart at the seams. Fourth, following those contacts, some changes in the direction of the modernized patterns will take place—*but not necessarily successfully.* It is necessary to insist on attention to the italicized portion of the fourth proposition. I am not at all sure the prognosis for the firstcomers is good, but for the latecomers the prognosis for success with modernization is so far very poor indeed.

From the perspective of modernization the nations, countries, societies, or areas of the world may be distinguished as follows: (1) The firstcomers, those cases where modernized patterns apparently developed slowly over a long period of time and with no previous models before them. The main examples are England, France, and the United States. (2) A large number of cases, especially European ones, whose peoples were in rather close contact with the firstcomers during the development. These are the early latecomers, if you will. I would include the Soviet Union in this category since I am not persuaded that the history of modernization there begins in 1917. (3) Other latecomers, most of whose people were, or were kept, largely out of contact with the modernized patterns of the firstcomers, and who came increasingly into contact with those patterns only after they were highly developed.

When one looks about the globe, the prospects of latecomers achieving high levels of modernization do not appear to be good. There are still European peoples who can hardly be described as highly modernized. Spain and Portugal certainly fit into this category, and how much of Eastern Europe over and above Albania still fits it is an open question. Japan, on the other hand, is clearly one of the more modernized nations and apparently will shortly become one of the most modernized, if not *the* most modernized one. Hence the fatuity of calling the process European or Western—quite apart from the geographical and historical idiocies involved. There is not a single modernized society on the continent of Africa unless one considers South Africa and Rhodesia to be cases. Even if they are considered modernized, both of these are clearly specific offshoots of the case of England. On the continent of Asia there is not a single highly modernized case, save for Japan, which is just off that continent. The Japanese case is a particularly interesting one, to which I shall have occasion to refer again and again, for she is the only twenty-four-carat latecomer who has shown any prospects of getting into the top five or ten most highly modernized nations of the world. If success with modernization can be called success, then Japan is the most conspicuous success of all. Australia and New Zealand are classified as highly modernized, but they too are specific offshoots of the case of England. In the entire Middle East there is only one case of a highly modernized society, Israel, and that is the result of the historical accident of plumping down a whole set of modernized people in an area where there is no reason to believe any such development would otherwise have taken place. The continent of South America has several cases that now approach high levels of modernization. Their development, however, is still markedly uneven—highly modernized urban centers while a majority of the population continues to live in relatively nonmodernized rural areas.

Thus as we look around the world, we see the firstcomers of modernization; we see the closely associated European satellite cases; we see the colonial offshoots of England; we see recent close approaches to modernization in the case of Mexico in Central America and in several of the South American cases; and we see Japan. At this point in time a larger proportion of the world's population lives in nonmodernized contexts than in modernized contexts—still! With such a picture holding into the latter part of the twentieth century, it is by no means certain that the world will become generally highly modernized, although I would maintain that it is extremely unlikely that any of the peoples affected by these modernized patterns will return over any broad spectrum of their operations to the status quo ante. How long they can persist in a sort of limbo of modernization no one knows. Some have been there for quite a while already.

The question of modernization is not, however, simply whether the nonmodernized will become modernized. There is another question: can the peoples who are modernized continue to live with those patterns? In 1972 uneasiness concerning the viability of our ways of life, let alone their aesthetic desirability, blows from many quarters. Can the modernized survive? Will they?

Leaving aside for a moment the limbo of modernization or the viability of the highly modernized, I would like to explain why I hold these patterns to constitute a universal social solvent. It is fashionable to discuss these matters in terms of the sins of imperialism. I do not care for what is usually referred to as imperialism any more than most of those who were influenced directly under it, but I think the question of imperialism is largely beside many of the critical questions about modernization. As indicated above, contact will be made by the people who have these patterns with those who lack them; when those contacts are made, disintegration of the status quo will begin; and some change—not necessarily successful—in the direction of modernized patterns will take place. All of this will take place regardless of whether the peoples concerned are forced by modernized peoples to do their bidding and the patterns diffused among them in that way. In this part I shall give reasons why these patterns will always invade once contact is made—why some attempt is always made, whether forced or voluntary, to take over some of those patterns—although that is not to say that that is the way in which the patterns of modernization did invade in each and every case. In individual cases these patterns may have entered their wedge by other means, but I shall give you reasons why they always would enter even if they were not introduced by other means. Throughout this book, reasons why the status quo is likely to disintegrate once the contact is made will be developed.

The Gist of the Matter for Latecomers

The built-in solvent effect of this modernization process touches heavily on something about which many are highly sanctimonious today. All over the world people distinguish between spiritual and material factors. Many like to argue that peoples can be distinguished by whether they are spiritually as opposed to materially oriented. Such discussions are usually more uplifting than sensible.

The following five generalizations about material factors hold:

1. There are no peoples, there never have been any peoples, and there never will be any peoples who fail to be aware of material factors.

2. There are no peoples, there never have been any peoples, and there never will be any peoples who fail to distinguish between being relatively better off and relatively worse off materially.

3. There are no peoples, there never have been any peoples, and there never will be any peoples who fail to prefer to some extent being relatively better off to being relatively worse off materially.

4. Peoples of the world do vary considerably—and this is what most of the sanctimony is presumed to hinge on—in the prices they are prepared to pay in order to be relatively better off materially. I think, however, the major difference that counts is the following one.

5. Peoples differ enormously in their horizons of the possible about being better off materially.

Whatever else you may say about the patterns of highly modernized peoples—and they may sometimes seem a dubiously gaudy affair—compared to any other historically known patterns of social organization, they are inordinately productive materially. Once contact is made between peoples who are possessed of these patterns and peoples who are not, the latter always see some possibility of material improvement by taking over some of these patterns—even if they are not forced to do so. It has been a frequent, not to say universal, conceit that, barring interference from others, people can take over just those patterns they prefer and leave the rest—combine the best of the East with the best of the West as some would have it—but the patterns never seem to come packaged in quite that way. That conceit and the error involved in that conceit have a lot to do with why the process is so subversive. It is, however, the readily perceived, inordinate material productivity, whether embodied in the sharpness of tools, the fire power of weapons, or the productivity per hectare, that always levers open the horizons of the possible.

This is not a theory of material or economic determinism as these are ordinarily discussed. I do not wish to maintain that humans live by bread alone. For the argument advanced here to hold, it is only necessary to maintain that a human never lives totally without regard to bread. No total ascetics survive. We may, I suppose, disagree on whether differences in the prices peoples are prepared to pay in order to be better off materially are more important than the ease with which one can pry open their horizons of the possible. My own interpretation rests on the latter assumption. I think the vision of the possibility of material betterment has been much obscured by ignorance and the absence of a habit of ingenuity. I do not think an appetite for material betterment has been severely limited by spiritual considerations for any save an ascetic few.

This book is built around four central points. First, modernization is a universal social solvent, and hence, however unsuccessful a people may be with this process, it is an utter waste of time to discuss whether or not they should be involved in it. Second, the main source of the subversiveness of the patterns of modernization when they come in contact with nonmodernized people inheres above all in the utter bizarreness of the everyday patterns that the highly modernized everywhere take so complacently for granted. Third, it is by no means well established that the bizarre patterns so taken for granted by the highly modernized are even viable patterns for human beings—certainly no large set of people has lived with them for very long. Fourth, none of the major structural features of modernization, as these features bear on either the problems of latecomers to the process or the possibility of firstcomers surviving what they have created, vary as dependent factors of the ideological clichés in terms of which they are ordinarily discussed. For most of these questions it is the level of modernization that counts and not whether the people concerned pledge allegiance to capitalism, socialism, communism, fascism, third-worldism, Maoism, or the new consciousnesses and cultures. Most discussions of such problems in terms of these clichés are wildly beside the point.

Special Problems for Latecomers

The whole field of modernization is understandably distorted by advocates reacting offensively or defensively against many of the bigotries and insensitivities of the past and present. For some the process of modernization is the same for everyone, and, of course, in some obvious sense this must be so since all of the cases are cases of modernization. At the opposite pole, there are those who feel that somehow you demean the dignity of the human spirit if you imply that the experience of one set of peoples either owes a great deal to, or has much to do with, the experience of others. This latter interpretation has splintered magnificently—usually along conventional ideological lines—but the lack of good solid sense in what is said has led to a sort of "ordinal" approach with references to the first world, the second world, and the third world scattered all over the place. That way of looking at the problem is better set up for indefinite extension than for enlightenment.

It makes a great deal of difference in many areas about which individuals and groups are deeply concerned whether a people or a country or a society is a firstcomer or a latecomer to modernization. When I speak of the firstcomers, I do not intend to imply that England or France or the United States or any other case that might be placed in this category developed this process without important interdependencies with other countries or peoples. Whatever those interdependencies were, however, the fact remains that these peoples did develop these processes at a time when they did not exist in any highly developed state anywhere else in the world. Moreover, save for a few prescient people (whose prescience was largely recognized in retrospect), these nations had no idea of where these processes would lead them.

The latecomers, on the other hand, live in a world in which the contrast between their own states and those of peoples who have passed the dividing line between the modernized and nonmodernized is one of the most important factors for them. There is no need here to spell out the special advantages of latecomers in this process, for these are already part of the common sense of our times. In the early part of this century Veblen spoke of the advantages of latecomers in being able to take over the latest technologies without the vested interests in obsolete equipment characteristic of peoples who had developed such technologies from scratch. The possible advantages in the sheer availability of knowhow—the examples, the experience, the range of possibilities

The Gist of the Matter for Latecomers

—are all spread before the latecomer, sometimes very rudely and in importunate fashion. In a rough sense you may even maintain that with the passage of time the facility and generalization of communication, both oral and visual, have increased exponentially, and have thus further escalated this type of "advantage."

There are, however, special disadvantages or, if you prefer a more neutral term, problems for latecomers to this process. I believe there are at least four such problems that can be classified as follows: (1) gaps and scale, (2) the lack of direct convertibility of assets, (3) running to keep up, and (4) coordination and control.

Before I take up the problems individually, Figure 1, illustrating the problem in general, may help us to understand better the general problems faced by all latecomers.

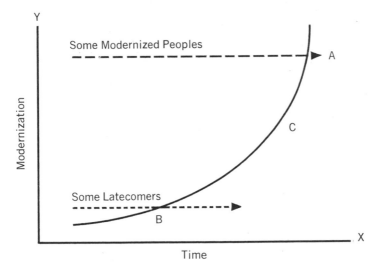

FIGURE 1

The X axis has to do with time and the Y axis with some index of measure of modernization—never mind for the moment what it might be. The curve is a sharply accelerating one. It starts out at very modest rates of increase, whatever those may be, and then, for the modernized societies and many of the latecomers as well, the curve becomes a very steep one—rates of change and development become very rapid indeed. The basic difference between the firstcomers to modernization, insofar as these can be lumped together, and the latecomers inheres not in the wickedness of imperialism or racism—however much these may have complicated the problems of latecomers—but, rather, in the fact that the firstcomers were able to march slowly up this curve in small steps over relatively long periods of time with no peoples further up the curve ahead of them. Depending on when you consider the process to have started, England and the United States had a hundred years or so to approach universal literacy and the general communications systems that the Japanese sought to achieve in decades. As indicated in Figure 1, the latecomers enter the curve at the point (B) indicated in dots whereas some of the firstcomers have already reached points on the curve indicated as A or C.

The Four Problems

GAPS AND SCALE

Now unless you are a mystic—unless the Gods did tricks for the firstcomers—they marched up this curve one step at a time, with most things starting out on a small scale and expanding as the process continued. Latecomers, however, if they are to get into the process at all, must take over some elements of technology and do some things on a scale that is a very far step removed from where their indigenous technologies and states find them. This sort of problem is conspicuously true of communication systems and educational systems. All of the latecomers to the process are faced with relatively low rates of literacy among their peoples. The Chinese and the Japanese were perhaps the most accomplished in these respects, but it is doubtful that the literacy rates in either country surpassed 30 percent of the population. Of course, literacy rates were probably much lower for the firstcomers to modernization when they began the process, but then those peoples had, depending on where you reckon those origins, somewhere in the neighborhood of a hundred years to make a major onslaught on these problems. (Incidentally, there is no reason to believe that the invention of printing, in Europe or in China several hundred years earlier, had anywhere near the impact on literacy that modernization has had [see below, pp. 99–100].) The firstcomers were also conspicuous for the fact that they developed their communication systems a small bit at a time, and we know that they paid dearly for this in the inefficient design of railroad systems and the like. Thus the latecomers must all strive to achieve relatively high rates of literacy and general forms of communication among the various parts and peoples of their countries quite quickly.

The gaps that latecomers must jump guarantee a considerable impact of strangeness. There is a sense in which what you make out of what you have at hand seems a great deal less strange than the totally new product that you import. One of the great advantages of latecomers is that they can import the means to jump those gaps. What they cannot import are the means to deal with problems of scale. There has been idiocy enough in all attempts at social planning for the latecomers to the process, but one thing that has not been idiotic has been the realization that levels of coordination and control required by these problems of scale alone generally represent an increase well beyond the

15

previous capabilities of the peoples concerned. I would like to defer the general discussion of the problem of coordination and control until later. The essential point here is that the problem of jumping gaps and of doing things on a much larger scale than has generally hitherto been the case presents not only intrinsic difficulties but also the difficulties implicit in the requirements for increased coordination and control.

Were Veblen still alive, he would have a field day with what several have labeled in his memory "conspicuous industrialization" or "conspicuous modernization." The mistakes that latecomers have made because of personal fascination with the extravagance of gold beds have surely been of small import by contrast with the insistence that everyone have a steel mill, that roads must be cloverleafed, and the like. The problems of jumping gaps and of doing things on an unaccustomed scale have been complicated by the feeling that somehow, surely, you are being discriminated against or are not up to the mark if you do not attempt to jump even greater gaps and do things on an even more magnificent scale than is either necessary or prudent, given the resources generally available and the values held by most of the latecomers. But the fact that many latecomers have eyes that are bigger than their stomachs does not change the fact that the stomachs that they must have for modernization are bigger than, and fundamentally different from, the ones they have had in the past.

LACK OF DIRECT CONVERTIBILITY

I repeat, unless you are a mystic, you must agree that the firstcomers crept up this scale of modernization one step at a time. They transformed their skills and material resources into those of the next level. They used their wrights, their blacksmiths, their carpenters, their woods and their metals, their grasses and their hides to make the machines, the materials, and the skills that were subsequently to be called the next stage. Many of the things that latecomers must have for the process cannot be directly converted from the materials and skills at hand. No amount of ingenuity or motivation can make a modern milling machine out of the materials and skills latecomers have at hand. The latecomers must turn to those abroad, even if those abroad do not force their attentions on them. Since they are latecomers, they have, of course, an advantage which the firstcomers did not; they can get help from abroad from people who are much more advanced in these respects than they are. This help can come in many forms: direct aid, forced attention, loans, and the like. Latecomers who are particularly wary about the perils of foreign indebtedness, as the Japanese were, may, especially if they have a fine appreciation of the economist's doctrine of comparative advantage, choose to do this by diverting available local resources to export activities. Even this route, however, poses problems far different from the kind of direct conversion that characterized the firstcomers. The vast majority of the productivity of the nonmodernized peoples has been locally oriented; all such peoples are characterized by quite high degrees of local self-sufficiency. While there have been notable exporters in history, the reorientation of any considerable amount of production at home for export, as is required by involvement in the process of modernization, constitutes in and of itself a radical reorganization of familiar ways of doing things and of looking at things.

Either way—whether simply searching the heavens and beseeching others for aid or carefully reorganizing and husbanding resources for international trade—modernization involves, as a minimum, an increased interdependency with others abroad. And that, of course, involves radical reorganization of the general structures of life, above all, at the local level, and that, in turn, has generally meant reorganizing farmers. Something well in excess of 80 percent of the non-modernized people of the world have been rural people for whom the major productive activity in terms of both income and time is some form of husbandry—usually agriculture. Even in those instances when, for considerable periods of time, these latecomers continue to farm, they farm differently under the new dispensations, and their production is differently oriented. With rare exceptions none of these peoples are habituated to the kind of neutrality about what they produce themselves or of what uses are made of their produce that we, who take modernization for granted, consider to be par for the course in a nonsentimental common-sensical world. For people who have had as a major goal very high levels of local self-sufficiency, even to do similar things with a larger view to exporting their resources is a radical change. Above all, the locals are unprepared for the enormous increases in interdependency involved.[3] The great difference in direct convertibility of assets is a problem to which the most

[3] Fei Hsiao-tung in his book *Peasant Life in China* (New York: Dutton, 1939) gives a wonderful example. An entrepreneurial genius in a small village in South China got the idea of setting up a crude "factory" in which the local girls could unreel silk cocoons. The enterprise prospered; the girls' wages went to their families; they no longer married early. Then came the 1929 crash and the depression. The major world market for silk was for silk stockings and silk underwear for ladies plus a certain amount for the affectations of U.S. mobsters—all luxury markets hard to explain to male undergraduates and now equally hard to explain to female undergraduates who have never seen silk stockings, although recently one of the latter allowed to me that she had seen some in her "grandmother's trunk" (the young are unaware of their greatest cruelties). In any case, this small village was tied into the world-wide depression as few other Chinese villages were. The villagers not only experienced depression, unemployment, and so forth, but they found themselves with a bunch of single young ladies who were over age and out of hand.

sophisticated among us tend, by our very sophistication, to be insensitive.

RUNNING TO KEEP UP

There is a certain irony to this problem, that serves as welcome relief from the dourness of the general subject. The advantages of the latecomers in having examples set before them are so obvious that it must be tiresome (especially to latecomers) to have them iterated. There is, however, also a special disadvantage to these examples. It is easiest to illustrate in monetary terms, though this is by no means the only sphere in which these disadvantages inhere. The gross national product per capita in the United States is now approximately $5,000 per year. In other words, if one took all of the goods and services produced in the United States in the course of a year and allocated an exactly even share to each human individual, regardless of age, sex, or previous condition of servitude, each share would come to $5,000. In a very good year—a year for singing—we in the United States achieve a rate of economic growth of approximately 5 percent. We would consider that a very good year, particularly if that were a real increase after discounting for inflation. If we had such a 5 percent rate, that would mean that the gross national product per capita would be 5 percent greater the next year.

In many latecomer countries the gross national product per capita is estimated to be in the neighborhood of $100 per year. Problems of how such things are estimated may lead to errors of as much as 100 percent, but even with a 100 percent error, that figure will still not be greater than $200 a year. Let us consider it to be $200 per year, and let us also consider for purposes of illustration that our little country X is the nicest little country in the world by standards relevant to such questions. The people of country

19

X know no extravagances and no idleness. They not only whistle as they work, but they work very well indeed. Let us even assume that their economy grows at the rate of 15 percent per year—something that is much easier to do when starting from a relatively undeveloped base, though in fact very few developing countries do anywhere nearly so well for all sorts of reasons. The only modernized people whose economy grows at anything approaching such a rate are the Japanese. For the Japanese a real rate of economic growth approximating 15 percent does not seem to be unusual; they are known to refer to a rate of 7 or 8 percent as being a state of depression. For any other modernized society, a rate of 5 percent is very good, and for any nonmodernized society attempting modernization, an economic growth rate of 15 percent, while by no means out of the question, is rare.

Leaving the extreme case of Japan to one side, however, look at the picture at the end of the year. In the case of the United States, the gross national product per capita has now risen to $5,250, if my arithmetic is correct, and that of little country X, whose people work so hard and make so few mistakes, is $230. From the point of view of many of the people in little country X, they are farther behind than when they started and made all the sacrifices and ad-justments that got them there. They started out $4,800 behind the United States, and at the end of a year of great effort they are $5,020 behind the United States. In cases of this sort it is an absolute waste of time to tell the frustrated people of country X that if they continue at this rate they will pass us. They would, of course, but from their own point of view they appear to have run very hard and fallen farther behind. The state of communications in the world, especially television, the movies, and the like, guarantee that they will be aware that their sprint does not seem to have gotten them as far as our stroll.

The irony of running to keep up will most probably turn

into tragedy if we are not able to give the runners at least the appearance of catching up to, if not overtaking, the leaders. In the world in which we live few people are going to have the wind for the race unless such a change as this is in prospect. There may be a special lesson in all this for those who feel that the solution to our ecological problems lies in our no longer being oriented to increases in productivity. If a fairy godmother were to wave her wand and remove this preoccuption from us tomorrow, the vast majority of peoples of the world would have to reconcile themselves forever to our present radical inequality of income distribution. Alternatively, a more equal distribution of what is currently available enforced on everyone would leave no one a great deal better off than the least advantaged among us today and would leave all of us facing a further decline. Instead, we had best seek ways of lowering pollution levels while continuing to increase productivity, rather than find surcease in a new piety.

INCREASED COORDINATION AND CONTROL

It has been one of the common-sensical clichés about modernization that for modernization to bloom for the firstcomers, some relaxations of centralization, some increases in laissez-faire arrangements, were necessary. Whatever may have been the case with firstcomers, that is not the case with latecomers. The whole question of centralization is not well understood. Most of us, impressed by individual acts of despotism in the past, have read into the past far higher levels of centralization than have in fact held true. None of the overwhelmingly centralized empires of history such as that of Genghis Khan have perdured, and those societies or countries or governments that have perdured have been combinations of some centralization and very substantial elements of decentralization.

I am not an expert on Vietnam (as the vast majority of

my colleagues seem to be these days), but there is one re-
frain about that area of sadness (given anyone's values) that
surely misconceives the question. On all sides we hear that
the vital infrastructure has been disintegrated by thirty
years of internecine warfare. No error could better beg the
question. The relevant infrastructure for modernization—
for any radical material improvement in the lot of these people—never existed. In many quarters this question is further
begged by the apparent solution to which it leads—that one
of the ways to solve the problems there is to restore the "old
hamlet (or village) spirit." The old hamlet (or village)
spirit cannot be restored. Were it possible to restore it,
moreover, the implications would be radically negative as far
as modernization is concerned. In all societies in the history
of the world, the old hamlet and village spirit has been overwhelmingly oriented to the maximization of local self-sufficiency and to a minimum of contact with more nationally
located centers. The ideal was to be let alone as far as
possible, rather than to be tightly integrated with the national scene.

Again, none of the overwhelmingly centralized empires in
history have long survived the death of the charismatic
leaders who generally set them up. This whole matter is
taken up below (see pp. 65–80). For the moment suffice it
to say that overwhelming centralization was never in the long
run feasible for logistic reasons, if not for others. Moreover,
overwhelming centralization was never necessary, save to
conform to the whim of a given political leader. There were,
after all, relatively few possibilities open to the general population, and the settings and activities of the overwhelming
majority changed relatively very slowly. When the process
of modernization sets in, however, regardless of whether the
process is desirable or moving efficiently or not, there is
always a need for more and different forms of centralization,

of greater coordination and control than have ever characterized the peoples before. I do not see how this can fail to follow from the three special facets of latecomers already mentioned above, but the need also inheres in the process itself. Seven decades ago Veblen was already describing modernization (he called it industralization) in terms of the "increasing delicacy of the interstitial adjustments" required for what he referred to as the "closely concatenated processes" of our modern world.

Over the long run, radical increases in coordination and control were certainly necessary for the firstcomers. Those increases, however, could and did come gradually. In the case of the latecomers, however, they are matters of urgency from the beginning. The previously existing forms of centralization characteristic of latecomers almost all require transformation as a minimum, and so far only the Japanese have shown themselves adept at making what appears in retrospect to have been an easy transformation. The problems of gaps and scale and conversion and frustration can, of course, be further complicated by "bad" centralization—and "bad" (that is, irrelevant and/or ineffective) centralization is extremely likely to take place. It does not follow, however, that the cure for "bad" centralization is decentralization. The probability is overwhelming that the cure for "bad" centralization is in all cases alternative possibilities of centralization (see pp. 65–80).

The screw of need for increased coordination and control is further tightened for latecomers by another factor that generally holds for them. As the need for increased coordination and control rises, it is overwhelmingly probable that the existing available sources of coordination and control will be simultaneously undermined in the process of modernization. There are many reasons for this, but one will suffice for the moment. For all of the nonmodernized peoples of the world, the last unit of decentralization of control has been the family unit. In the last analysis, one counted on control of individuals by pressure brought to bear on family heads or through some other closely identified kinship organization. For the vast majority of nonmodernized peoples —regardless of whether, as was true of the Chinese, they put family considerations ahead of any others—oriented most of their behavior to family considerations and spent most of their time in family contexts.

If there is one set of practices more vulnerable than any other to the process of modernization, it is the set of family practices characteristic of nonmodernized peoples. For example, all peoples everywhere experience their most intense initial learning in some form of family context. That is where everyone, with very rare exceptions, learns to walk and to talk, to eat and to sleep, to control bodily functions, to interact with other human beings—to be a human organism. Unlike the peoples of modernized societies, the peoples of nonmodernized societies, however, also learned practically everything else that they were expected to do for the rest of their lives from older members of their own families, usually from their fathers and mothers. It is hard for modernized people to envisage the extent to which such dependency and habituation reinforced the control of older family members over the young. We modernized people do not ordinarily consider ourselves to have been "educated" in a family context at all. The things we do regard as having been learned at home we don't regard as education. Indeed, we tend to be increasingly insensitive to the extent that even "character" is formed at home.[4] Education, we think, occurs almost exclusively in terms of school, despite the fact that we have in common with the vast majority of all

[4] There is an ambivalence about this, however, since we prate a great deal in Freudisms.

other human beings who have ever lived the fact that the steepest part of our learning curves—the learning we do between birth and, say, three years of age—the learning on which all other learning rests, occurs overwhelmingly in family contexts. Thus far, the development of day-care centers and kibbutz-type organizations has certainly not made any major dent in this as far as the population of the world is concerned, though perhaps it may in the future.

And so it is that one of the very first side effects of contact with the modernized is that the nonmodernized learn something of great importance and learn it from persons who are not members of their own families. As soon as they do, some of that old hold is gone. While it is possible to give other reasons why in particular cases the previously prevailing patterns of coordination and control characteristic of latecomers to the process will disintegrate upon contact with modernized people; the one just mentioned applies to all and will do for illustrative purposes for the moment. However many reasons one may give, the lesson is clear: at exactly the time that the level of coordination and control required mounts out of all comparison with the previous experience of the peoples concerned—as interdependency accelerates—the available means for coordination and control come apart at the seams.

Three Special Cautions

From the above, three special cautions follow. Apart from simple ignorance of the facts, I believe that almost all of our failures in trying to plan for and help latecomers can be seen as examples of a failure to comprehend one or some combination of these three cautions.

First Caution: The requisites for modernization are not

necessarily the same as the prerequisites for modernization. (Translation: the things that have to be done to keep a modernized society modernized are not necessarily the same as the things that have to be done to get it there.) In trying to understand the problems of latecomers to the process, you cannot look at the things one has to do to keep England, the Soviet Union, or the United States going and infer directly that that, therefore, is what one must do if country X is to get there.

Second caution: The prerequisites for firstcomers are not necessarily the same as the prerequisites for latecomers to the process. (Translation: for reasons discussed at some length above, the things that the firstcomers had to do to become highly modernized are not necessarily the things that latecomers have to do to get there.) As a minimum there will always be different problems of timing and scale.

Third caution: The prerequisites for one latecomer are not necessarily the same as the prerequisities for another. (Translation: the things that one set of latecomers has to do to become modernized are not necessarily identical with the things that have to be done by another set of latecomers.) The process of modernization for latecomers consists essentially of two sets of elements: those elements that inhere in the process of modernization as such and those elements that inhere in the historical basis from which change takes place for a given set of peoples. That historical basis, including as it does special geographical, ethnic, and heaven knows what other endowments, is never identical in any two cases. The elements that inhere in the modernization process as such, on the other hand, are for most of our present purposes highly similar. The main difference among latecomers, therefore, rests largely in their differing historical backgrounds. The things that the Japanese had to do to become modernized are not necessarily the same as the things that the Chinese have to do to become highly modernized. Lyrical, mystical humanism to one side, no other sets of elements inhere in these processes. This is why no presently achieved progress in the social sciences—not in economics and demography, which have gotten somewhere scientifically and certainly not in anthropology, political science, and sociology, which have not—is a substitute for historical literacy about the peoples concerned. Such historical literacy about a people concerned is, alas, never accomplished by acquainting oneself with the last five or ten years of their history. Almost always, to understand these problems, one must go back to the last relatively stable period *before* the changes under discussion took place. For most peoples of the world today that involves at least a rudimentary acquaintance with the history of their past 100 to 200 years. One colleague has suggested that one reason why so many of our economic aid programs in Latin America have failed is that we have consistently tried to devise programs and program "styles" for Latin America as a whole rather than trying to tailor them to individual countries.

The reason these cautions are especially necessary inheres in the fact that: (1) some of the requisites for modernization are the same as the prerequisites for modernization; (2) some of the prerequisites for firstcomers are the same as the prerequisites for latecomers; and (3) some of the prerequisites for one set of latecomers are the same as the prerequisites for another set of latecomers. For example, the achievement of high rates of general literacy is necessary in all these cases. How it is done and at what rates it must be done vary enormously. The trick is to differentiate those things that do hold true for all cases from the major lines of variance among them. In Part II of this book I have tried to emphasize some common peculiar features of modernized peoples and to give some sense of why they are

27

so disruptive of the latecomers—especially when they are introduced suddenly with no great sensitivity by the modernized as to how bizarre—how atypical—their patterns are and no great sophistication by the latecomers as to where the implications of those introductions lead. The emphasis here is therefore on features of modernization that pose inescapable problems for all latecomers. Treatment of the special problems of different latecomers requires more time, space, and knowledge than are available to me.

PART II

How Peculiar Are the Modernized!

I N the preface to this volume I stated that the argument in this book proceeds largely in terms of those things all social beings seem to have in common and those traits and ways of doing things that characterize nonmodernized as opposed to modernized people. The latter always appear as a sort of overlay on the former. Understanding that such an overlay exists (including, of course, a more detailed overlay for each specific set of people) is all that is required to reconcile one of the supposed paradoxes that frustrate the social sciences—the paradox that says, on the one hand, that all human beings are alike and, on the other, that no two human beings are the same.

From the tone of the above it should be clear that I regard a considerable part of the literature in this field as mistaken, misleading, or silly. Alas, very little of it is rash. Rash thinkers can make fruitful errors; silly thinkers cannot. In Part II of this essay I have tried to separate out the general features of modernized societies that distinguish them and the people who live in terms of them from the commonalities of all the people who lived before them, including those from whom they descend directly. It is also my contention that those features account for the universal subversiveness of these patterns when they are introduced—no matter how—into nonmodernized contexts. Finally, it is my contention—call it speculation, hypothesis, or belief as you prefer—that these are the very same features that probably call into question or at least stimulate curiosity about whether this peculiar set of highly interdependent patterns can persist—whether people can continue to behave so and survive. Thus I make no attempt to discuss here the patterns on which human systems in general depend—those are taken for granted as the background of such a study. A systematic analysis of whether these modernized patterns are viable ones for human beings would require a systematic and rather lengthy analysis of the implications of these patterns for those patterns that could be called requisites for human life. The argument here rests primarily on the bizarreness—the peculiar nature of these traits or patterns considered individually. That bizarreness alone is enough to raise a presumption that their introduction will be wildly subversive of the status quo of the nonmodernized. Nor does it require a Cassandra to wonder whether the very recency of the flowering of these patterns does not raise the question of how long the blooms can last. I note that the latest fashions in the social sciences and the general discussions of these matters in our press and that of others—the preoccupation with imperialism, racism, and exploitation—make little if any reference to the matters discussed here as the most critical ones. They may be right. I wish the problems were as easy as a contest between the wicked and powerful against the good but helpless could be.

Finally, I have distinguished twelve categories of patterns here: (1) education for an unknown future, (2) fast change versus slow change, (3) strangers, (4) exotic organizational contexts, (5) high levels of centralization, (6) the use of money and the distribution of income, (7) the relation between towns and villages, (8) education for modernization, (9) recreation and politics, (10) a sexual revolution, (11)

32

relationship aspects, and (12) demographic changes. In each case the bizarreness of the modern patterns is asserted and illustrated. If these patterns are as unusual in human history as I allege, that alone would be enough to arouse curiosity at least about their strategic nature. There is, however, another factor. In individual cases in history it is possible to find instances of one or more of these patterns usually affecting some highly restricted segment of the population concerned. But what is never found among the nonmodernized is this set of patterns taken together and considered as a highly interdependent whole. There is not space here, and alas not talent enough either, to trace those interdependencies in any substantial detail. I have merely tried to arrange them in such a way that threads from one to another will be obvious enough even if the nature of the weave is vague.

This last consideration, of course, poses in a very special way one of the major policy problems facing us, both with regard to the latecomers to modernization and the present-day survivors of the process. Should we decide to eliminate one or two of the patterns referred to here—say, increased centralization or the rapidity of change, or a peculiarly unstable set of relationship patterns—in order to avoid beastliness for latecomers or insure happiness and tranquility for ourselves, we won't be able to do it. Cutting out one or two of those will not merely leave a hole in the fabric; the fabric is not woven that way.

Before discussing the exotic ways we take for granted, and by contrast what I suppose many would refer to as the "normalities" of human life, I would like to make one sociologese distinction. That is the distinction between *ideal* and *actual* patterns. The term "ideal" as used here has no moral or ethical implications. When I refer to something as an "ideal pattern" or use the word "ideally" or the phrase

33

"ideally speaking," I simply mean that the people to whom I refer feel that is the way things should be done. When I refer to "actual patterns" or use the word "actually" or the phrase "actually speaking," I mean simply that that is the way the individuals concerned are in fact behaving.

This is an important kind of distinction if you wish to understand human beings, and, incidentally, some rather powerful generalizations about human beings can be stated in these terms. Ideally speaking, bullying is considered a bad thing in the United States. We side autonomically with David against Goliath. We do not take David to task for a wily departure in weaponry and tactics. It is enough for us that he was smaller than Goliath. We don't stop to reflect that Goliath may have had problems—always big for his age, a bit slow, laughed at by the other Philistine kids. No, for us, Goliath was a bully. Actually speaking, it comes as no surprise to any of you that a certain amount of bullying does take place in the United States. Ideally speaking, I suppose, the vast majority of faculty members of our universities are true intellectuals and are not snobs. Actually, in this time and day, if you mean by an intellectual one for whom the life of the mind is uppermost, intellectuals constitute only the tail end of the distribution of university faculties and, whether we are intellectuals or not, almost all of us are highly developed intellectual snobs even though we may be unaware of our snobbery. Other examples also come readily to mind. I think the form of slavery characteristic of the United States is the worst that the world has ever seen—not because the levels of brutality visited upon individual slaves were unprecedented, but rather, as noted in the Preface of this book, because the United States setting, as far as I know, is the only case of slavery carried out by people who had simultaneously as one of their ideal patterns that all human beings were created equal and should be treated accordingly in certain broad minimal respects.

How Peculiar Are the Modernized!

The distinction between ideal and actual patterns is in one sense well-known through time. Social scientists as well as laymen have always made such distinctions. Nevertheless, almost no attention has been given to this distinction as one of the most powerful tools at our disposal. Very powerful and illuminating generalizations can be made in these terms, and probably no social phenomena can be understood without some reference to them explicitly or implicitly.

Here are six propositions, in these terms, which hold true for all peoples past, present, and future:

1. There are no peoples, there never have been any peoples, and there never will be any peoples who fail to distinguish between ideal and actual patterns—between the way in which they prefer people to behave and the way in which they in fact observe themselves and others to behave. There are, for example, no peoples who never correct their children. There are no peoples who have no norms, no values.

2. The ideal and actual patterns for a set of people as a whole never coincide perfectly. There may, of course, be individuals who never bully others among a people that holds bullying to be a bad thing, but there are always some who do bully others some of the time.

3. To some extent the people concerned are always aware of the fact that ideal and actual patterns do not coincide perfectly. The sensitivity of individuals to such discrepancies varies enormously, but there is never a situation in which no one ever says "I wish he hadn't done that," or "He shouldn't have done that." Doesn't it go without saying that there are, of course, many cases of discrepancies of which individuals are generally if not totally unaware?

4. To some extent some individuals are upset by the failure of ideal and actual patterns to coincide. Some discrepancies between ideal and actual patterns constitute a source of stress and strain for all known peoples.

5. Some of the possibilities of integration inhere in the fact that the ideal and actual patterns do not coincide perfectly. This is not paradoxical relative to Proposition 4 above. Some of the ideal patterns, for example, are mutually inconsistent. Some of the possibilities of adjusting as well as is done inhere in the levels and types of discrepancies.

6. Cynics of the world to the contrary notwithstanding, discrepancies between ideal and actual patterns can never be accounted for solely in terms of hypocrisy. There is certainly enough of the latter, but virtuosity in hypocrisy is probably as rare as virtuosity in anything else. To be a virtuoso of hypocrisy, for example, one must also be a virtuoso of rationality and self-awareness. It is a frequent naiveté of the very young, the very romantic, and the very sentimental—not to say the very idealistic—to hold that, when people do not in fact behave in a way called for in their ideal patterns, they are simply insincere about those ideal patterns. The problems that inhere in such discrepancies would be a good deal easier were this the case, for all of these cases would then fall under Levy's Fourth Law, which holds that one should "always pray that your opposition be wicked. In wickedness there is a strong strain toward rationality. Therefore, there is always a possibility, in theory, of handling the wicked by outthinking them. Corollary One: good intentions randomize behavior. Subcorollary One: good intentions are far more difficult to cope with than malicious behavior. Corollary Two: if good intentions are combined with stupidity, it is impossible to outthink them. Corollary Three: any discovery is more likely to be exploited by the wicked than applied by the virtuous."

In one form or another, knowledge of the ideal-actual distinction is part of general human thinking, and characteristically it is one of the most neglected parts. Many apparently contradictory observations turn out to be no longer contradictory if you distinguish with some care whether the observations refer to ideal or actual patterns, and many things that have been taken as gospel turn out to be quite false and misleading when you consider them carefully in these terms.

Take, for example, the many descriptions by travelers, missionaries, anthropologists, sociologists, and geographers of those people who presumably have plural wives (the so-called polygynous peoples). We have endless descriptions of such peoples, and most of these appear to hold that the peoples concerned get married at roughly the age of puberty, near the age of, say fifteen for both girls and boys. By implication, if not by direct assertion, it is generally held that almost all of the little girls and little boys get married, and that the little boys have two or more wives. All such descriptions mislead ingenuously. It may not be true that every little child that is born into this world alive is "either a little liberal or else a little conservative," but with very high probability, indeed, every single one is either a little male or a little female. There are very few exceptions to this, and those exceptions are not significant statistically. For all human environments on which we have any information whatsoever, the ratio of those little males to those little females at birth is of the order of 102/100. In some recorded cases the ratio is as high as 107/100. It certainly averages out to no more than 104/100. The little males are less viable than the little females after birth, as they are apparently *in utero*. As the little males approach age fifteen, the ratio of little males to little females must approach 100/100; that is to say the ratio approaches one. Under these circumstances, if the little boys are to have two or more wives, the people concerned must do something interesting, such as kill off 50 percent of the boys or have the girls marry at age fifteen and the boys marry at, say, age thirty or thirty-five. This latter will give them a bulge of females. Unless they do something like this, or steal females from some other set of peoples, which simply leaves them unmatched, plural wives cannot have been generalized in any population in world history. If you are interested in survival of the human species, this is probably, on the whole, fortunate. Most peoples in past history have, after all, lived on the margin of demographic subsistence, and, never mind male vanity to the contrary, as the number of females per male goes up, their fertility declines. When the sultan has four hundred ladies at his disposal, it is not remarkable at all that he has eighty or ninety children. Had those ladies been distributed, one to a husband, they would, in the same period of time, probably have had at least 1,600 or 1,800 children—most of whom would not have survived, but many more than eighty or ninety would have been about at any given point of time. The descriptions of peoples with plural wives describe the ideal patterns characteristic of many peoples. When such ideal patterns are present, some minority of the males in fact achieve them. They are the elite of that society. There have been no truly polygynous peoples as those have generally been described, though there have been many for whom polygyny is an ideal pattern actually achieved by only a small percentage of the male population.[1]

[1] It can be easily shewn, as the mathematicians say, that there have also been no cross- or parallel-cousin marriage systems as those have generally been described. In fact most of the anthropological and sociological literature on kinship and the family is seriously in error and importantly misleading because of failure to distinguish between ideal and actual kinship patterns. Given the fertility and mortality rates and the sex ratios characteristic of most of humankind, only 12 to 15 percent of a people could get married if each had to marry her or his cross or parallel cousin. The large extended families so often ascribed to the Chinese rarely existed for a very simple reason: few individuals long survived the birth of their first grandchild and rarely did more than two children per marital pair survive to maturity. This is not an error of the inept. The inept have been taught it by the best of our talent.

How Peculiar Are the Modernized!

Closely connected with this is a form of radicality about which no one has done any speculation to speak of, but it is one that may face us tomorrow. It has long been known that whether a little child is born into this world alive as a little male or a little female is a function of whether the human ovum is fertilized by an X chromosome-bearing sperm or a Y chromosome-bearing sperm. Ever since this was known, it has been the dream of some to be able to separate those sperm out in such a way that anyone could determine the sex of offspring at will at conception. We now have cheap and effective means of birth control and will surely get better ones. If this other discovery is made—and it could be made momentarily—if the process is cheap and at all consistent with human dignity, one of the dreams of humankind, the easy control of the sex of offspring, will be readily at hand. When this happens, we shall all of us be up against two other generalities about human affairs: for all known peoples, the males have always expressed an overwhelming preference for male offspring—and so have the females. With such a discovery, that ratio that has been roughly one to one throughout history could easily jump in the direction of ten to one. Long before it got anywhere near there, we would see radical changes of a sort rarely envisaged for humankind. Incidentally, it would solve the problem of the demographic explosion very rapidly, indeed, unless the desire for numbers of offspring per female increased at the same or somewhat higher rate than the preference for male offspring. Since this seems unlikely, not only would the population explosion cease to be a danger, but the extinction of humankind might become a lively possibility. Of course, the preference for male offspring might be affected, but those affectations are probably going to lag and will apply to preferences for sex of first child last.

Some of the still unpublished work on fertility by Professors N. Ryder and C. Westoff raises questions about the degree of preference for males over females, especially among modernized people. Even they, however, find a strong preference for a male as a first child. If their work is correct, the radicality to which I point would take longer to develop, but it would certainly develop. Only a finding to the effect that easy, cheap, dignified choice of the sex of offspring does not affect the hoary ratio of one to one would alter the basic hypothesis presented here and reiterated at the end of this book (pp. 144–146).

There are two main reasons why everyone should be careful about the distinction between ideal and actual patterns. In the first place there is a great tendency to confuse ideal and actual patterns—a tendency to speak of ideal patterns as though they were actual patterns or to speak of actual patterns as though they were ideal ones. As indicated above in the case of polygyny, such confusion can be misleading. In the second place, it is overwhelmingly probable that when you read about a people or when you ask them about their patterns, you will get your answers in terms of ideal rather than actual patterns. This is not because those particular people delight to deceive you. It is rather because the ideal patterns are always simpler than the actual patterns, and they are the ones which are taught. It is overwhelmingly likely that if you ask anyone to describe an organization —even one she (or he) happens to dislike—she (or he) will describe it in terms of the ideal patterns of the organization rather than its actual patterns. Everyone is well advised, therefore, in all that she (or he) hears or reads about a people to ask whether the patterns referred to are the ideal ones or the actual ones—to what extent these coincide and to what extent they do not.

There is one final question to be raised about ideal and actual patterns. In all past history many ideal patterns continued viable as ideals because factors over which people had no control kept nonviable ideals from being tested. The generalization of poverty avoided testing the belief that increases in income would solve most problems. The nature of mortality reinforced filial piety by ensuring that there be few children to turn out badly and few adults to survive to senility. Faced with material affluence and longevity as only two of the relevant factors associated with modernity, we may for the first time have posed a massive new challenge to our ideals. Our problem may not be, "Can we approximate our ideals?" Our problem is much more likely to be, "Can we live with our ideals when we do approximate them?" How ironic if longevity, wealth, and peace prove as difficult for humans as caducity, poverty, and war.

1

Education for
an Unknown Future

One of the most extraordinary things that we take for granted is education for an unknown future. As the history of humankind goes, nothing could be more unusual than that. One of the popular minnesingers to the young tells the audiences he delighteth to flatter that they, as teenagers, must, as all teenagers before them, redefine the world for themselves. One of the major difficulties facing them—the one he fails to help them with—is that redefining the world is precisely the sort of thing that young people have rarely if ever had to do before in the history of the world. Certainly never before has that had to be done by the vast majority of any peoples' young.

Always in the past, before our modernized societies developed, the overwhelming majority of all individuals have in fact had very short-range futures—life expectancy at birth averaged from perhaps twenty-five to thirty years or so for most of them, and for those who survived to age twenty, their life expectancy was only slightly over thirty-one or thirty-two years. But they had a very long-range view of the future—both their private futures and the general social future. They expected the future to stretch indefinitely before them just as it had for their parents and their grandparents and their great grandparents. What may be even more important is that, as noted above (p. 25), they expected to learn practically everything about that future that spread before them from older members of their own society—most especially from older family members. We, however, now live in a world in which an increasing number of people have very long-range futures (life expectancy at birth is well in excess of seventy years for most highly modernized people), but we have a very short-range view of the future. We expect substantial change—in less than two to three decades—and we get it.

For the middle-aged this is easy to recognize even if difficult to understand and adjust to, especially if they grew up in relatively sheltered, sedentary backwaters of a highly modernized society. I grew up in a rather small town, Galveston, Texas, a town in which my father before me had been born and reared. I well remember hearing as a child stories of the Galveston of his childhood, and I remember thinking that I would never be able to convey my sense of the great difference to my own children since their childhood would never differ from mine as much as mine had from his. But when I speak to my children of my own childhood, they count me to be marvelously imaginative, though neither particularly reliable nor credible. I speak to them of automobiles on wheels with wooden spokes and with running boards —at a time when no one could have dreamt that a rumble seat might someday connote transportation to gang warfare. The first electric phonograph in our house is still a clear memory for me—as is radio when they had genuine comedians like Billy Jones and Ernie Hare, "We're the Interwoven Pair," who sang songs like "What Kind of a Noise Annoys an Oyster, That's the Kind of Noise That Annoys Me."

43

Only Arthur Godfrey and I remember them! There was no television. Most of the roads, even between major population centers like Dallas and Galveston, were dirt roads, and anyone who traveled as much as 150 miles, let alone 200 or 300, on any one of them without a puncture boasted and exclaimed about it for weeks. The college entrance crisis was virtually unknown to either parents or children. When I tell of these marvels, I might almost be talking to my children about T'ang Dynasty China.

The problem of educating children for an unknown future is an interesting one if you do not permit yourself to be frightened out of your wits about it. How are you to do it? How are you to prepare the young for a future that you cannot or do not predict? How are you to counsel them? How can you even discuss their problems with them? Most of us, in discussing anything with the young, do so in terms of double distortion. The first distortion has to do with our memory of what it was like to be that age. Our memories are not likely to be perfect in this respect. The other distortion inheres in the probability that even if we had perfect recall, what we would recall would not be highly relevant to many of the problems faced by the young today. What can you do when you encounter even a whine to the effect, "How was I to know?" How, indeed, are they to know? Who is there to tell them? I do not agree with those who seem to hold that it would be wicked to tell them even if you knew, lest it scar their creative impulses, but we are not in general facing that problem. So far as we know, none of us has visited the future and returned to tell the tale.

The problem of educating children for an unknown future is also one of the best examples of the truly subversive nature of the modernization process. In this connection modernization is most subtly awful. Clearly, this is a problem for the already modernized people—for the survivors of modernization. Rapidly changing technologies and increasing rates of interdependency are all a part of that problem, but latecomers too emphatically have to educate their children for an unknown future. This is one of those things exported to the latecomers well in advance of other associated aspects of modernization. With communication systems still barely developed, new educational practices hardly begun, with a vast majority of the population still living in rural areas, and manufactures only piddling, the latecomers still face a revolution in their ways of life as radical as they can undergo. Nevertheless, even though virtually all of the ordinary common-sense indices of modernization may still be low, the universal solvent effect of modernization—the fact that many of the patterns of the status quo always disintegrate, literally, even if the peoples concerned are not successful in becoming modernized—means that those peoples are suddenly faced with educating their children for an unknown future. They even have to do this before the life expectancy at birth of those children is great. Though this in a literally terrible way may be a merciful aid, it is ephemeral and rapidly wiped out by a decrease in mortality, especially of those who will have to live longest with an unknown future.

It is a matter of great pride for most of us that ours is an age of change. There are an increasing number of savants in this field who would make this circularly true by defining modernization as the easy adjustment to rapid change. Under the sway of the patterns of modernization we are the first peoples for whom in general the term "old-fashioned" has become an epithet—except for the collectors, exquisites, and the like among us. Even the squares are for change.

It is especially dramatic to phrase this as a problem of educating the young for an unknown future, but the problem is a great deal more pervasive than that. I put it that way only because we ordinarily think of education primarily in connection with the young. One of the peculiarities of highly modernized societies and of latecomers to modernization is that we must *all* learn how to educate everybody, including ourselves, for an unknown future. There is every reason to believe that the learning curve for all individuals is sharpest in the earliest years. Individuals seem to learn more and faster then, and it seems not unreasonable to assume that the ability to learn flattens out as one grows older. The excellent memories of young children, which are not characteristic of them when they mature, may be a function of the fact that in the early years so little is stored in the memory that the problem of recall is minimal. This sort of possibility alone would lead to the expectation that people would be less adept at learning as maturity wore on. In highly modernized contexts and in the context of latecomers to modernization, however, we must continually educate and re-educate not only the young, including in that the children, the adolescents, and the young adults, but we must continually educate and re-educate the middle-aged and the aged. After all, never before in history did a sufficient percentage of those born survive long enough so that some form of compulsory retirement had to be learned for the vast majority of all individuals born.

Here again, very interesting problems inhere in the highly modernized context. As the Chinese increase life expectancy at birth to something in excess of seventy years, they may constitute the first people ever to be faced by the problem of how to handle a situation in which there may be as many as 100 million senile individuals among them. Unless modern medical technology is capable of eliminating senility before life expectancy at birth in China reaches seventy years, we shall see a day in which if senile Chinese are wheeled four abreast past a given point, their procession will never end. Until modernization held us in sway, senility was an episodic individual problem. It was not a part of the life cycle for any save an exceptional few. Under modernized conditions those virtuosi of old age who avoid senility will be the exceptional few. Many if not most of the glories of filial piety rest on the fact that very few of the younger generation have had to cope with the senility of the older generation. With modernization all of us will have to find a way.

The education of the young and of their elders has another peculiar characteristic in modernized settings. Figure 2 illustrates a hypothetical learning curve for human beings.

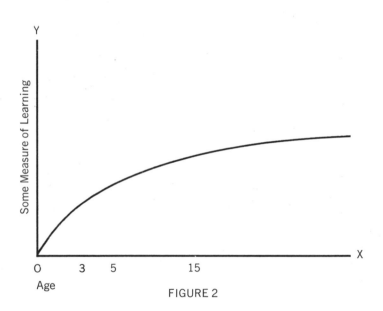

FIGURE 2

On the Y axis there is some sort of index or measure of the amount of learning and on the X axis there is a measure of time, or the life span of the individual. As mentioned above (see pp. 24–25), the early part of that curve—and I think there is every reason to believe that it is the steepest

47

part of that curve for the great majority of all individuals who have ever lived—is lived out overwhelmingly in family contexts by the vast majority of all individuals past and present. That is certainly the part of individual learning on which all subsequent learning is superimposed. The individual learns these things (see above p. 24) in a context that is not specialized with regard to this kind of education. This is only one of many functions performed in family terms. The organization concerned is generally referred to by some such term as "family" and not by a term such as "school." A school is a much more highly specialized form of organization. Although many functions other than education take place at school, a school is regarded as overwhelmingly concerned with education. Isn't that still an ideal pattern anyway? Schooling in this sense has gone so far in modernized contexts that we ordinarily refer to schools when we answer questions concerning education. If I ask, "Where were you educated?" you will most likely tell me where you got your highest degree, from a college or university. If pushed, you will tell me where you went to secondary school, and subsequent to that, primary school, and the younger among you will tell me where you went to nursery school, whereas the older among you will probably stop with your kindergarten.[1] It will not occur to most of you,

[1] We have all become captives of one particular kind of academic snobbery that almost certainly costs us a good deal and others a great deal more. The United States is probably the leading case of this. It is the more important in the United States since she is the first society in the history of the world in which a college education or its equivalent has touched any but a small minority of the population. Until the U.S. case developed, probably no society ever had as much as 5 percent of its youth so affected.

The academic snobbery in question takes the following form. Other things being equal, it is more prestigious to teach in any university or college than in any secondary school, in any secondary school than in any primary school, in any fifth grade than in any fourth grade. If the learning curves at all approximate the one I have used for purposes of illustration, we can hardly escape the odd implication that we give the highest rewards in terms of income, recognition, power and pelf of all sorts to those who teach our young in the flatter parts of their learning curves. (Of all with whom I have discussed this, only one, a mathematician, has observed, "Why not? It's harder to teach them there.") There is a sense in which we may be able to afford this. After all, the overwhelming majority of all of our teachers have themselves passed through some form of higher education. We certainly pay some prices for this. The better teachers are in the earlier grades, the greater is the probability that they will not continue to teach there. There is certainly not any a priori reason to believe that she or he who teaches well in the early grades will teach better in the later grades. If there are individuals who have a comparative advantage in teaching at one level as opposed to another, we would certainly be very much better off educationally speaking if our systems of rewards and motivations were more carefully calculated to reinforce those comparative advantages.

If amount of educational experience has anything whatsoever to do with teaching ability, we at least discriminate as we do among people all of whom have had something of the order of magnitude of twelve to sixteen years of educational experience, including four years of higher educational experience. But this academic snobbery of ours has been exported to virtually all of the latecomers to modernization. For them too, other things being equal, it is more prestigious to teach in any university than in any secondary school, in any secondary school than in any primary school, in any fifth grade than in any fourth grade. But for them there are few teachers with sixteen years of educational experience. The higher the level of experience of the teachers, the greater is the probability that they will teach in the higher grades. It may, however, be true that a second or third grader struggling with the problem of attaining literacy taught by a teacher hardly more than literate herself (or himself) may be far more radically disadvantaged than an eleventh grader whose teacher knows less than she or he might about chemistry. Many of the cynical among us would maintain that the entire U.S. educational system—especially our university system—is a demonstration of the fact that, the more advanced the student, the better able she or he is to cope with inferior teaching. If that is the case at all, latecomers to modernization pay a terrible price for the importation of our academic snobbery. Our academic snobbery may in effect have substantially flattened the learning curves of their children.

unwarned, to tell me that you were ever educated in a family context, and, therefore, by inference you imply that all that basic initial learning is not part of your education. This is not just a play on words, however. The fundamental difference between modernized people and most of the other people in the history of the world is that the latter have not only acquired their basic initial learning in such contexts, but, with relatively few exceptions, they have also acquired all other learning in such contexts or very closely related ones (such as neighborhood or village organizations or male clubs or lineage groups, and the like).

The children of some of the elite members of nonmodernized societies learn many things in contexts that we would regard and classify as schools. And the same may be said of those in training for the priesthood in many orders, but these have never constituted more than a very limited percentage of the total population. Until the process of modernization had gone far in the world, the vast majority of all people who ever lived, learned practically everything they learned in social contexts that were not specialized for educational purposes. In almost all cases they learned from people who were in fact older than they, who were representatives of older generations than they, and with whom they were going to continue to be in contact after the education took place. Other things being equal, it was overwhelmingly probable that those very people would be the ones who held power over them and were responsible for them. When the organizational context in terms of which this took place was not a family context, it was overwhelmingly likely to be a neighborhood or cooperative organization very closely associated with family contexts.

Let me reiterate: the vast majority of all the people who ever lived learned everything they could learn for living from older people who had gone through it—they learned about a known future—and they probably learned it from older members of their own family. Unless we achieve a level of social predictability that may constitute the worst tyranny of all, that will never be true again for the world as a whole and will increasingly cease to be the case for those people for whom it presently holds. The future will increasingly be a world in which everyone is educated for an unknown future in' highly specialized contexts womaned and manned by strangers—except for that initial early learning that most humans have shared in common.

It has not been proved or, as far as I know, even alleged that schools can and will keep up with the rapid changes in and additions to the basic knowledge that seems to be a requisite of modern societies.[2] No one knows whether schools can do the job, but no one even dreams that this knowledge can be bestowed on children generally in family contexts. Almost overnight with modernization we have come to doubt, by default if not by ideal, that parents know best or can teach it successfully if they know it.

[2] It is currently fashionable for both professional educators and those who claim expertise by virtue of being parents, or merely being interested, to claim that the asserted failure of our schools is that we must convert our schools to new and vital functions. Rarely can you find any one of these who has ever posed the question: insofar as our schools fail, do they fail because (1) we have not been trying to do the right things; (2) we have been trying to do the right things but do them very poorly; or (3) some combination of the first two?

51

2

Fast Change
versus Slow Change

Prior to the development of modernized societies the world has seen many changes, but until modernized societies developed, change has usually been and been perceived as a jerky, discontinuous, or slow process. Even when humans have imposed cyclical theories of change, as a sort of special intellectual tour de force, those cycles have been ones of very long phase. For most of the history of humankind rapid change was almost synonymous with catastrophic change, and both were likely to be synonymous with war and pestilence. Otherwise, the pace of change was overwhelmingly likely to be slow, even if it were in some sense unremitting and the changes radical. Not so for the people of modernized societies. As indicated above, the revolution of modern medical technology has greatly increased the future of humans at exactly the point in time that humans have come to have a short-range view of the future. We take rapid far-reaching social change—and technological change is only a special case of social change—for granted. As I indicated above, we boast of the fact that our children will live out their lives in a different world than the one in which we grew up. We are so extremely accustomed to rapid rates of far-reaching change that we have grown inured to change. Many far-reaching changes take place without our being aware of them or regarding them as far-reaching changes. For example, it was not many years ago that I first heard an advertisement on television in which a major automobile manufacturer held forth the idea that his automobile was "the ideal second car." I had just gotten accustomed to the fact that universal car ownership was being taken for granted; by now, of course, the two-car family is an accomplished fact, and the three-car family unit is well advanced.

The conservationists still act as though lumber and public utility companies are the major threats to our public lands. While those threats may be dire enough, we in the United States already live in a country in which something in excess of twenty million families can realistically envisage the possibility of owning a second home. That number may very quickly increase to well over thirty million families. Since upward of 80 percent of all our families presently live in urbanized or suburbanized environments, the average conception of an ideal second home is likely to be something quite unpretentious—say five acres of land removed from others with a little brook running through it. That quickly adds up to 100 million acres without a single additional access road or path. The home-away-from-home may turn out to be a worse curse than a second or third automobile.

This matter of taking rapid change for granted is simply another way of looking at the problem of having to educate children for an unknown future—of having to educate everybody for an unknown future. Never before has change been so taken for granted. Few things could so upset our present status quo as stagnation. There are ironies associated with all this. So accustomed are we to far-reaching change that we often regard as inseparable two quite separable possibilities. The first of these is radicality of change—the extent to which any given change generally alters the conditions of life of those who undergo it. The second of these is violence. Indeed, there are many today who link radicality of change and violence so inseparably that they give every appearance of feeling that the former does not and cannot take place without the latter. For many, the term "revolution" means just that combination; a usage that is certainly based on the dramatic awe in which we still hold the French Revolution. One of the most interesting things about the French Revolution, however, is that it is one of the relatively rare cases in history in which radical change in general social structure has in fact been tied to high levels of violence. Throughout the history of humankind an argument can be made that high levels of violence have on the whole been more conservative than revolutionary. Some of the bloodiest conquerors of history are more notable for the numbers of people they killed and the extent to which their conquests colored the map than they are for any alteration they brought about in the lives of those who survived them.

Modernized people come to take continuous radical change for granted. Latecomers are forced to cope with radical changes whether their participation in the process of modernization is of their own volition or is forced upon them. The problems of latecomers not only mount as radical changes take place for them, but they also seem to mount further insofar as they have difficulty encompassing certain forms of radical change. It is not true that all forms of change are good by anybody's standards. In the process of these changes, especially for latecomers, somebody always gets hurt, and it always occurs to somebody that "things were better in the good old days." Some people always attempt to cope with these problems by fundamentalistic reactions, but they are never successful. You can't go home again; death appears to be the only escape from this Chateau d'If too.

It is all very well to talk about a modern human's unusual

54

ability to cope with change and even to define her or him by that unusual ability, but surely there is some upper limit on a human's ability to adjust to rapid radical changes. If we presently undergo radical social transformations roughly once every quarter century and gear our education for an unknown future to such a rate of change, can we up that rate to once in two decades, to once a decade, to once a year. . . ? One of the questions about which we rarely speculate and know nothing definitively is the following: What is the upper limit—to what rates and scales of change are human beings capable of adjusting? Right now most of us speak of the problems of modernization as though we mean the problems of *becoming* highly modernized. The problems of staying highly modernized and simultaneously staying alive in any bearable way of life may be much greater. Our ecological threats may only scratch the surface.

3

Strangers

When I address an audience of modernized people without forewarning them, I often ask them how many strangers they have encountered so far during the course of the day. The answer is likely to be "no one in particular," or the number of strangers mentioned is likely to be small. Yet if by strangers you mean people unknown to you, with whom some sort of contact has been made, the actual number is likely to be in the hundreds or even in the thousands. Thus most of the people in the audience will have driven somewhere earlier in automobiles. Often, when traffic has been flowing smoothly, they have interacted with literally hundreds of strangers at combined velocities in excess of 80 or 100 miles an hour and combined masses in excess of two tons. The lack of abrupt physical encounters under such circumstances is not a trivial matter. When you consider that ordinarily you have had no previous known contact with the individuals with whom you interact in traffic, it may be even more remarkable that there are as few traffic fatalities as there are rather than that there are so many.

One of the most curious things about us is that we take fleeting casual contacts with other human beings completely for granted. That has never been true of any substantial proportion of any population before our modernization developed. The vast majority of people have known who strangers are and have had relatively few contacts with them. It makes professional social scientists—anthropologists and sociologists especially—a bit angry if one puts it this way, but it is nevertheless not a great distortion to maintain that the vast majority of all peoples who have ever lived have had a very simple attitude toward strangers: "You either fete 'em or eat 'em!" The important thing is that strangers are recognized at once. Almost to a person nonmodernized people assume that the overwhelming majority of all their contacts with other human beings will be contacts with people previously well known and easily placed by them. The advent of a stranger is an event.

This has been true enough in rural settings with very low densities of settlement. It has also been true in the great urban settings of nonmodernized societies. Even when these cities were quite large and involved hundreds of thousands of individuals, most of the individuals lived most of the time in sections of the city in which they carried out the vast majority of all of their activities. You can see survivals of this in so modern a city as Tokyo today. Things are still arranged there by districts such as Roppongi, Toranomon, Seimonmae, and so forth. In those districts one does not ordinarily find building or house number 25 next door to or across the street from number 26. It may be in an entirely different part of the district, since numbers were at one time assigned on the basis of the order in which the buildings were built rather than where they were located. This is perfectly sensible if everyone can normally expect that the majority of the people moving about in the district will know approximately the order in which the structures were erected. This, however, implies no large number of strangers. Today when such districts do have large numbers of strangers moving in and out of them—in all those districts—there appear numbers of bulletin boards with special maps of the district so that strangers can locate the places they seek.

Most modernized people seem to feel that if you walk into an area and have contact with people you have not met before—if you behave decently and with the proper respect for others—that decency will be reciprocated, and that the relationship may be as easily broken off as it was begun. But the vast majority of nonmodernized people living in highly self-sufficient—usually rural—areas are not at all prepared for such adept making and breaking of relationships.

The vast majority of all relationships for all people in nonmodernized contexts have been based overwhelmingly on who a person is, regardless of whether what she or he were capable of doing were considered at all. Such considerations are by no means unknown for modernized people. The modernized, however, take it for granted that they shall also frequently consider people not on the basis of who they are, but rather on the basis of what they can do that is relevant, regardless of who they are. Still, even for us, the modernized, a considerable number of our most influential relationships are based on considerations of who a person is. The overwhelming majority of all members of all societies including the most modernized receive their initial placement and their initial influences in a kinship context—especially a family context. That context is overwhelmingly determined for all peoples by who an individual is and not by what she or he can do. I am someone's child because of who I am and not because I have behaved properly or improperly.

For those people who are accustomed so overwhelmingly to dealing with people on the basis of who they are, the question is how is a person to decide that in the case of a stranger? Specifically, one of the things you do not know about a stranger is *who* she or he is. In the course of divesting her or him of that mystery, she or he ceases to be a stranger. Highly modernized people in an enormous proportion of their activities feel no explicit compulsion to pierce this veil. We are content to take fleeting casual contacts for granted without knowing more about the identity of the persons concerned than that they do not drive on our side of the road if they are coming from the opposite direction. We are content to identify them by what they do rather than by who they are. Sexists though we all are, we frequently don't even differentiate strangers by sex. Even among us, who take fleeting casual contacts so much for granted and who nevertheless initially learn most of what we learn in a context of relationships based on who an individual is, there is no convincing analysis or study of how we learn to take fleeting casual contacts for granted. How many and what proportion of such contacts can an individual adjust to? We do not know. No substantial proportion of any population in the history of the world took fleeting casual contacts with strangers for granted until well into, if not the latter parts of, the nineteenth century. Most of the people who do adjust to that today did not adjust to it until some time well into the twentieth century. Is there a limit on living with strangers, and, if so, what is that limit?

4

Exotic Organizational Contexts

Humankind in their ingenuity have distinguished two types of organizations. There are and always have been, for all peoples, what in technical jargon are considered to be multifunctional organizations—the term is both jargonal and somewhat misleading. These are organizations that are not overwhelmingly oriented to any one particular performance or type of performance. Their members take it for granted that large numbers of different types of things will be accomplished in terms of them—and that, above all, no one of them alone determines the general character of the organization. All of us are familiar with such organizations—families, neighborhood organizations, friendship units, and the like.

Another type of organization is a highly specialized one. Many different things are done in terms of these organizations *too,* but overwhelmingly their members are regarded as being properly concerned primarily with a single type of performance. In ordinary language these are referred to as economic organizations, political organizations, educational organizations (schools), and the like. It is not true that humans do not struggle for power in terms of economic organizations or allocate vast sums and resources in terms of political organizations or seek relaxation and reputation as well as knowledge in terms of schools. Nevertheless, these organizations are regarded as having their primary area of concern in the economic sphere, the political sphere, the educational sphere, and so forth.

Here again, modernized humankind are unusual. We not only create such organizations, we also literally take action in terms of thousands of these highly specialized organizations for granted. We operate in terms of the other less specialized kind of organizations too, and consciously we do not ordinarily even differentiate strongly between them and the specialized ones. Sometimes we even speak of the family as though it were highly specialized and likely to be as evanescent as we take our specialized organizations to be. But that is far from likely to be the case. Indeed in one sense the family has probably become a great deal more important for the modernized. The nonmodernized were fully known by all in virtually all their circles. With our highly compartmentalized lives in terms of our highly specialized organizations, the family unit has become the sole "castle of the me."

The overwhelming majority of nonmodernized people were quite different. In the first place they acted out their lives in terms of a very small number of organizations, indeed, and most of those were of the first type. Rarely, if ever, did they act in terms of the second type at all. As modernized people, we take these strange, highly specialized organizational contexts for granted—just as we take fleeting casual contacts with strangers for granted. These two things are obviously closely related. We could not operate in terms of thousands of highly specialized organizations unless we were accustomed to fleeting casual contacts with strangers. Not only do we not count on knowing who drives with us or against us on the highways, but we do not count on knowing the people who sell us things, who collect our taxes, who run our railroads, or even who teach our children.

The special importance in all this of schools has already been alluded to above. We take specialized educational organizations—schools—so much for granted that we do not in a common-sense way consider education to take place except in such contexts. When we do recognize that it takes place otherwise, we tend to give it the aura of this specialization. We refer to the "school of hard knocks." We refer to "experience as the best teacher," and for us teachers teach in schools. Our images for learning come from this specialized context—and not usually, especially not consciously, from the family context in which we, in common with all other human beings, learned the vast majority of everything on which all subsequent learning is based. Very few if any of us learned the fundamentals of being human in a specialized context. We learned those in a family context as did all of the nonmodernized people, with very few exceptions. They, unlike ourselves, learned practically everything else in such contexts as well. With contact with modernization, that is quickly disrupted.

The average individual accustomed to our modernized ways of living has no conception of the number of organizations in which she or he in some sense participates—or how odd she or he is in not having any idea of how queer that is. Most of us don't even have any conception of how many stores we patronize. The vast majority of all nonmodernized people had a very clear sense of the organizations to which they in some sense belonged—and of the ones to which they did not belong.

Closely involved in this is another peculiarity of our ways.

Exotic Organizational Contexts

We take it for granted that joining and leaving many such organizations can be as fleeting and casual a matter as those contacts with strangers we take for granted. It ordinarily never occurs to one of us that the fact that we have never purchased a hamburger or a milkshake at this particular stand before will pose any sort of a problem for us. We assume that we will order the hamburger and the milkshake; they will prepare it; we have a fairly clear idea of what they will be like; we will pay for them in a currency that they will recognize and readily accept—and they and we have never seen one another before and need never see one another again.

We carry these customary performances with us wherever we go. Whenever we try to help others in less modernized areas, we tend to act on such bases autonomically. If there is something special to be done—especially if we do not want it mixed up with anything else—we set up an organization to accomplish it. If we wish to dig a well, we form a group just for that purpose. Isn't that the simplest way to do it? Doesn't that get everything less mixed up than alternative ways? Cuts down on red tape, huh? What could be more natural? Almost anything—if you mean by natural: ordinary, to be expected, par for the course. While these exotic organizational contexts have been known in many nonmodernized societies, the range of their development and the numbers of individuals who acted in terms of them were usually very restricted indeed. With the advent of modernization—as the solvent does its work however fitfully and unsuccessfully—the proliferation of these exotic organizational contexts becomes prodigal.

Modern humankind are frequently regarded as suspicious and even cynical, and yet, without a moment's hesitation or thought, we trust our lives to strangers and rely on organizations for the simplest and touchiest needs of our everyday existence. We are usually astonished, and the more angry for our astonishment, when those faiths are betrayed. Almost any country bumpkin of the past would consider himself a fool to act so, and surely well in excess of 90 percent of all the people who have ever lived in the past were just such country bumpkins.

5

High Levels
of Centralization

From childhood on, all of us have heard stories of kings
and emperors, of the terrible despots of the past who in
the twinkling of an eye could do as they pleased—raise the
low to high and dash the high to dust—the wishful thinking
of our kings and emperors. We are naive. As stated above
(see pp. 22–23), no empires of the past have lasted long
if they were very highly centralized. The Chinese emperor
could no doubt scrag any individual he wished, but the fact
of the matter is that he did not try to control individuals
directly. In general he had no need to. The logistics of
nonmodernized societies made overwhelming centralization
impossible, and the patterns of behavior in general made it
unnecessary. None of the attempted overwhelmingly centralized empires—almost always those of the great military
conquerors—long survived the death of the charismatic
leaders who founded them. When they did survive, it was
by diluting those patterns of centralization and returning
to previously decentralized allocations of power and responsibility. The day-to-day domination of individual activities
was hardly necessary for any purpose at hand. After all,
these people were educated for a *known* future; they and

their leaders had very long-range views of the future. Farmers were not likely to have much leeway in what they planted, or when they planted it, or how they planted it, or what they did with it once it had been harvested. Under such circumstances it is not necessary to have people standing by to tell an individual what to do. You know what she or he is likely to do most of the time.

Furthermore, the high levels of local self-sufficiency meant in most cases that if someone locally did something disastrous, the disaster was not likely to spread beyond local limits. The delicacy of interstitial adjustments of the closely concatenated processes of which Veblen spoke was virtually unknown. Today they have become vulgar. In the past a specialist usually had to invent things for such relationships to become critical—close-order drill or minuets or elaborately formal gardens—but general social relationships were not ordinarily delicately poised.

For most of us centralization is regarded as villainous, and I do not wish to argue that matter one way or the other. It is one of the facts of life that levels of interdependency get higher and higher and higher as modernization proceeds. The probability of any given disruption spreading its effects to all parts of the system increases accordingly. The matter is a ticklish one because it is so closely tied to the topic of "freedom" about which we like to think humankind feels so strongly (though most of past history for most of humankind does not bear this out). In all discussions of "freedom," sooner or later, someone iterates that, of course, no one should be free to shout "fire" in a crowded theater when there is no fire. Those of us who most permissively decry any interference with the creativity of ourselves or others, in general, assent to this. Even Existentialists generally agree with this. As life becomes more and more highly modernized, however, it becomes increasingly interdependent. And as it becomes increasingly interdependent, the number of things that constitute the equivalent—or are deemed to constitute the equivalent—of shouting "fire" in a crowded theater when there is no fire mounts exponentially.

All the modernized societies of the world seem to be getting more and more highly centralized. Many of the less highly modernized societies of the past would appear on the surface to have carried centralization much further in certain respects than seems to have been required by the levels of modernization so far achieved. But over the long run, the more highly modernized societies become, the more centralized they become. Of course, for most of us the problem is complicated by the demographic question. It is estimated that a doubling of our society's population will take place within sixty years or so, and the rate of doubling for the United States is relatively low as these problems go and may get lower. If that population were to be distributed in exact proportion to its present distribution (that will of course, not be the case; it will bunch in some places more than in others), will not traffic have to be more carefully regulated? Will we not all have to pay closer attention to when and how we can and cannot move about? When I first moved to Princeton nearly a quarter of a century ago, we had traffic jams only on special occasions such as football weekends. Now we have two a day almost every day—one in the morning and another as most of us leave work. Our traffic is far more centralized now than then.

The romanticism that surrounds this subject is hard to penetrate. One of our favorite fantasies is that the solution to "bad" centralization—that is, to forms of centralization that are demonstrably inefficient and contrary to easily agreed upon criteria—is decentralization. That is *never* likely to be the case. The solution to "bad" centralization is much more likely to be alternative forms of centralization—whether anyone likes it or not.

Arguments on this score are usually conducted in child-like fashion. Someone is sure to say, "Wouldn't you agree that too much centralization is a bad thing?" I agree, and I add that *too much* lettuce will kill you. That is what we mean by "too much." We are not given a priori any clear criteria for what constitutes *too much* centralization. The amounts we seem to need to scrape by escalate continually.

Many of us, who hate and decry centralization the most, also decry most what we as moderns have done and are doing to the environment and one another. And we seem to see no inconsistency in calling for a decrease of the one and the cessation of the other. Yet, clearly, unless a fairy godmother waves her wand for us, the cessation of our environmental despoilment, let alone its redress, will require enormous increases in the regulation—even the *regimentation*—of what we may and may not do. Local citizens' action groups have, alas, a very poor track record. Besides, for most of our most serious problems they would be as inefficient as backyard blast furnaces were.

Presumably, one of the major buttresses of our freedoms is the decentralization implicit in state and local governance as presently constituted. Is it though—even by default and inefficiency? There is not a single major problem confronting us on either the domestic or the international front that does not have its solution impeded by state and local governance as presently constituted. State and local governments as presently constituted in the United States are clearly obsolete and are certainly badly centralized by most of our standards, though probably too little centralized as well. The fact that we cannot get away from local outlets does not mean that we must have high levels of decentralization.[1]

One of the most difficult problems facing latecomers to modernization has to do with an increase in effective centralization, an increase in coordination and control—an increase in the ability to cope with a constantly accelerating rate of interdependency at exactly the point in time that the existing bases of coordination and control are being undermined. Even if none of the existing patterns of coordination and control disintegrated rapidly during the process of modernization, the latecomers would still be faced with the problem of creating new devices and conceptions of handling their peoples and regulating and regularizing the relations among them.

Before, the locals could be pretty much left to themselves; now they must be melded into the new nationals. Before, family heads could be relied upon to call deviants to account; now there must be some concept of accountability to the state. The modernized take it for granted that the

[1] Centralization increases even where decentralization is planned —perhaps especially so. Much of the popularity and advocacy of revenue sharing is based on the romance of decentralization. Regardless of whether Rep. Wilbur Mills has his way or not, revenue sharing will increase centralization. Very quickly it will erode local and state bases for levying and collecting taxes and probably with good riddance—by most criteria a more wasteful, inefficient, uneven, and unfair system would be hard to devise. In addition, however, no matter what protestations are written into the legislation about leaving the decisions for use unfettered in local or state governmental hands, the first defalcations or general scandals about applications of these funds will bring irresistible demands for supervision, with or without Mr. Mills. Does anyone really think that over the long run the buccaneers of, say, a lone star state will be permitted to loot the ship as they please or that a given state can use the funds to perpetuate segregation? Mr. Nader alone has too many helpful elves for that. Revenue sharing will mark the true end of state and local public finance, no matter what all the proponents say.

state or nation or government will have a monopoly of the legitimate use of force; the nonmodernized do not. The modernized do not ordinarily equate a change that gives the government—or merely moves it toward—a monopoly of the legitimate use of force as centralization, but it is that and a big new concept to boot for most of the nonmodernized.

The latecomers have to create infrastructures where nothing previously existed. In a situation in which large numbers of people are likely to get hurt and even larger numbers to be frustrated for one reason or another, it is necessary to do things that fly directly in the face of one of the most fundamental biases characteristic of nonmodernized people who wish to be interfered with as little as possible at the local level. It is not so much that these people feel that "he governs best who governs least," but rather that "he governs best who governs most locally."

Preference for local self-sufficiency is not to be equated with hatred of hierarchy. It is very difficult for a person of my biases—and these I share with most academics, intellectuals, women, and men of goodwill, etc.—to face up to the fact that human beings in general adjust far more readily to hierarchy than to egalitarianism. In all human history only one type of relationship that is egalitarian by ideal is common to humankind—friendship. For all societies friendships are distinguished, and ideally all parties to the friendships have roughly, if not identically, the same rights and responsibilities. Actually, of course, friendships frequently do not conform to their ideal patterns. As far as I know, no other organizational context emphasizing egalitarianism, even ideally, is common to all or even to a large number of different societies. There may be a certain survival value in the overwhelming acceptance of hierarchy, however much violence that may do our sentiments about freedom. Any relationship that is based on such egalitarianism is subject to fracture at the whim of any member or members at any time. This simply will not work for any relationships whose continuance is important for survival. The larger the numbers involved and the more critical the purposes are deemed to be, the less practical friendship is as a device. We may all like to believe that the (an?) essence of human is freedom, but the (an?) essence of society is hierarchy. Well over 99 percent of all human relationships in history have involved some element of hierarchy. Homo sapiens is also homo hierarchicus. Actually down through history the achievement of egalitarianism and freedom has been primarily an elitist preoccupation of individuals who have had every reason to believe they would more than hold their own under such dispensations. Our loftiest expressions about freedom have had undertones of " 'It's every man for himself and God for us all,' said the elephant as he danced amongst the chickens." All this in no way implies that every hierarchy is a good one—or even a useful one.

The rapid increases in centralization that are characteristic of modernized societies pose another of those problems of limits faced by modernized peoples. Just as there is a question of what are the upper limits of rates of change to which people can adjust, there is the question of what are the upper limits of levels of centralization with which people can cope. Throughout most of their history humankind have adjusted to relatively low levels of centralization. Overnight—as history runs—in the last century to a century and a half humankind has been asked to adjust to constantly increasing rates of centralization.

The higher those rates of centralization go, the greater is the strategic relevance of knowledge—the higher the level of centralization, the greater the importance of adequate social planning. Here we may be faced with one of the special dilemmas of modern peoples. In the second and third decades of the twentieth century, when knowledge of the new physics was just being disseminated to the layman, the Sunday supplements used to be full of the possibility that humankind would die the death of entropy. One week the Sunday supplements said that we would die by burning, and the next week they were likely to say that we would die by freezing, but however they viewed the entropy death, it was some billions of years away. We thrilled to it, but we did not worry very much about it. In more recent decades we have been worrying about the fertility death— the possibility of drowning in our own population increase. Now we have added to that the general ecological threat. I am somewhat more frightened by the possibility of the *stupidity* or *ignorance* death. As our levels of interdependency grow higher and our levels of centralization and even regimentation increase to cope with it, the greater is the probability that the implications of any error in our planning will spread catastrophically to all parts of our world. Mistakes in the war games of brinkmanship, given the nuclear weapons at our disposal, are probably the most obvious example, though perhaps more controllable than others. Finally, we are becoming increasingly aware today that failures to know how to attain agreement on national and international means to halt, let alone reverse, ecological disasters may doom us all. Wringing hands over these matters does not involve any increases in centralization, but any effective means for dealing with any of them certainly would; that, in turn, will further increase the need for new knowledge—and lots more of it.

We do not have great reason to be sanguine about the progress in the social sciences or, indeed, about alternative possibilities of applicable knowledge about human affairs. If the amount of knowledge of that sort available to us falls markedly below what we need to carry out the planning implicit in the levels of centralization that we must have—the avoidance of catastrophe will become solely a matter of luck. Everyone who prates about probability is well aware of the fact that she or he has a field explicitly because "luck" is so exceedingly rare. If we are not able to increase the rate at which we acquire such knowledge— quite apart from any sentimentality about our technical knowledge outrunning our moral knowledge—we shall die the stupidity death.[2]

[2] When this matter is discussed someone always raises the possibility of decentralization based on self sealing loops—that is, systems so arranged that feedback from one to another is minimal. Quite apart from the prices in general necessary to construct such systems, there is still the question of the regimentation necessary in a modernized context to convert our systems to such systems. I would not, however, have you think me irresponsibly snide about our hopes for decentralization. Professor Charles Frank has stated as good a case as I know for decentralization, and I have with his permission included it here:

I would argue with your assertion that increasing centralization is a universal critical pattern of relatively modernized states. I would not refute the fact of increasing centralization of some (but not all) kinds of decisions, but I believe it is misleading to focus on centralization as the critical pattern variable. Certainly, interdependency increases very greatly as the modernization process proceeds. This does not mean, however, that in order for interdependencies to be taken into account, decisions must be more and more centralized. Increasing interdependence means that the rules of the game under which individual decision-makers operate must be modified, mainly in the direction of imposing increasing restraints on individual and group behavior. But there are good rules and bad rules—good rules allow for a large degree of individual and subgroup autonomy while taking into account interdependencies in an efficient fashion. In the economic sphere the price system is a very efficient mechanism for taking into account interdependencies and for insuring that individual decisions are at least consistent with each other. The increasing use of money, which you correctly point out is one of the important aspects of the modernization process, leads to an increasing tendency to value things in terms of money. Money prices and changes in money prices provide signals that enable interdependencies to be taken into account without requiring the

Given the inescapable overtones of authoritarianism, regimentation, and ordering, whenever one discusses problems of centralization, it is hard to escape some foretaste or aftertaste of armed forces. Except as a focus for distaste, armed forces until quite recently were in general a neglected subject treated primarily by specialists on military affairs as such and by people who write about Genghis Khan, Napoleon, and our Civil War. Even now the interest is more likely to be pejorative and limited than taken for granted and general. In many settings of history, and most especially in our own, there has been a general distaste for the subject on the part of the civilian population and a special distaste for it on the part of the academic experts. In the United States setting there has been a further special limitation since we and the British seem to be practically unique in considering our armed forces overwhelmingly, if not solely, a means for the external purposes of offense or defense and in ignoring the other universal use of armed forces for the internal maintenance of order. In the United

---

centralization of decisions. I can cite case after case in which a decentralized procedure, making use of the signals that are available through the price mechanism, is measurably more efficient than systems of centralized decision-making and control. This is the kind of thing that economists deal with all the time, and I would argue the major contribution of the economic sciences can be found in the theories that assert the efficiency of decentralized decision-making procedures using price systems and in the policy recommendations based upon theories of this sort.

Even where price mechanisms are not available to assure the efficiency of decentralized decision-making processes such as, for example, the State Department bureaucracy, I would argue that it is possible to devise rules of the game that insure that interdependencies are taken into account in any acceptable way that allows for significant individual discretion and decision-making power. In fact, I would come down on just the opposite side as you, and assert that in most cases where centralization is recommended as a means of solving problems, the solution to the problem is more likely to be found in better decentralization rather than further centralization.

States we are only just becoming aware of this second element, which so many before us have taken for granted.

We begin to see now increased concern over the role of armed forces in problems of modernization quite apart from their use to enforce the patterns of modernization on peoples other than one's own. Armed forces are likely to be quite strategic with regard to problems of centralization as a whole and with regard to the particular problems of coordination and control that are so very great for latecomers. All moralizing to one side, it is overwhelmingly probable that the latecomers will insist on maintaining armed forces—for the internal maintenance of order, if for no other reason. In addition, the latecomers are likely to go to considerable lengths, even including universal conscription, in the effort to get the very best human power, both physical and mental, for service in their armed forces. The latecomers are also likely to be extremely anxious to acquire the lastest equipment and techniques for use by the members of their armed forces. They are sure to want them to be effective and ready regardless of whether they envisage their use for the internal maintenance of order or for the external purposes of defense or offense vis-à-vis their neighbors. Thus it is better than an even money bet that armed forces on a considerable scale will in fact be maintained in all of these cases, and we know that such maintenance carries a high price tag. Finally, other things being equal, the armed forces are overwhelmingly likely to be the major pool of administrative capacity and talent —both of which are in short supply and critical for latecomers.

If one is not captive of the ignorance that holds the distinction between civilian and military to be a legitimate use of the law of the excluded middle—if one does not insist on thinking in terms of the military *versus* the civilian —there are, however, some possibilities with regard to usage of armed forces. Contrary to many of our biases, armed forces are not difficult to control. Except under conditions of quite general social disintegration, the problem of controlling armed forces is not a problem of dealing with mass mutinies. Rather, it is a problem of coping with palace revolutions likely to be carried out by young officers' cliques, sergeants' cliques, or the like. These violations fall under Levy's Fourth Law. Problems of this sort are ordinarily kept to a minimum and handling them is facilitated by the fact that, for reasons that are by no means entirely clear, in armed force contexts the general maintenance of disciplined organization is taken for granted even when poorly executed.

There is another thing about armed forces, however, that is especially relevant here. In addition to this stress on discipline and even blind obedience, the armed force of a nonmodernized people, other things being equal, is likely to be that segment of society that puts the greatest stress on: (1) rational behavior, (2) selection on the basis of relevant merit (objective recruitment), (3) strictly defined and delimited performances (limited liability), and (4) dealing with people without a personal involvement with the individual as such (avoidance). All of these emphases are also highly stressed in the process of modernization in spheres in which never before has much been made of them—especially spheres such as employment, government, communications, and the like (see below, pp. 121–126). The extremely practical earthy focus of armed forces makes such emphasis relatively simple even in nonmodernized contexts. Even when only the sons of the nobility were eligible to joust with one another, the victor was not determined by social heredity. Moreover, in nonmodernized contexts it was only in the armed force setting that those who proved themselves incapable of thinking rationally were likely to be wiped out by death. The first wave of the flower of French knighthood who charged the English longbowmen at Crecy were randomly selected for stupidity —but the second wave. . . . Finally, in most of the history of armed forces their leaders have been well aware of the fact that once you have the armed forces gathered together, when they are not needed for the direct exercise of force against others, you are much better off if you keep the members busy most of the time doing something of which the effects will be visible and, if possible, regarded as constructive.

The greatest barrier to the general use of armed forces during modernization processes is our general inability and/or unwillingness to think in terms of the *nonmilitary uses of the military*. Military people seem to feel that this will take the edge off the military, and the nonmilitary frequently feel that the attempt to do so will simply result in the military taking over everything. The latter need not be a threat (or will be less of a threat) if one understands the general problem of maintaining control of armed forces and also understands that the problems of governing a people are quite different from commanding an armed force. Whenever commanders of armed forces try to take over a people, they have to subordinate command to governance if they are to be successful.

One sees many examples of the nonmilitary use of the military in the world today, and there are even striking examples that are not generally considered as such. One dramatic case of nonmilitary uses of the military has to do with the state of Israel, for example, the use of the military to repair the educational gaps of Jews from certain Middle Eastern areas. There has undoubtedly been a great deal of this associated with the Communist regime in China, especially with regard to agrarian production, although in recent years there are some signs of a swing back toward more conventional views of armed forces. One hears allegations of cases in Latin America from time to time, and most guerrilla leaders claim that that is exactly what they do with their own armed forces. One of the most dramatic cases of the nonmilitary use of the military oddly enough has in fact occurred in the United States, where in general it is difficult to get anyone to discuss the subject or any of the possibilities without first bowing your head to a long series of epithets about militarism and the like. Until the last two decades or so—long before anyone dreamt of seeing the military-industrial complex as the genius causing our difficulties—practically every major public works project, especially those having to do with communications, transportation, and control of rivers, was mediated by the United States Army Corps of Engineers without any notable military takeover in this sphere. The Corps may not have scored nearly so high ecologically as hindsight would require, but the Corps hasn't gotten out of hand—hasn't come to dominate either government or industry. Even in our current talk about the military-industrial complex the United States Army Corps of Engineers is rarely accused of either personal aggrandizement by individual members or aggrandizement of power by the Corps as a whole. Insofar as it can be correctly said that we are a militaristic nation, no one has yet alleged that our militarism is a function of the fact that the largest nonmilitary use of the military we have so far made is our use of the U.S. Army Corps of Engineers.

In modernized contexts we probably pay dearly for failing to make nonmilitary uses of the military.[3] The latecomers

[3] There is a great deal of talk about the importance of improving conditions in the ghettos and improving the general state of the environment. Yet nonmilitary uses of the military in this con-

to modernization, however, are never affluent enough to afford to keep their military forces solely for military purposes. Besides, those military forces offer latecomers another possibility of coordination and control. One of the greatest problems latecomers face is that the new influences spread so rapidly and so readily that the indirect effects

---

nection are almost never considered. We may be neglecting possibilities. For example, many would agree that people who are forced to live in the ghettos, who have already been brought up there, have systematically learned to fail. Almost all of our proposals for developing environments in which such people can learn to succeed systematically are premised on the fact that in those environments they will learn to succeed by clambering over the backs of their fellow disadvantaged unsuccessfuls. Even when special environments are created to take them out of the ghetto environment that has something to do with their problems, they are likely to find themselves there only with their fellow disadvantaged—save for those in charge. Alternatively, universal conscription of females and males aged seventeen to nineteen would create an environment in which these individuals could learn to succeed systematically and be away from the environment that has something to do with their problems. Furthermore, since they constitute no more than 15 to 20 percent of the relevant population, given universal male and female conscription, they could be so distributed in this environment that they need not succeed by clambering over the backs of their fellow deprived, and the system could be biased in favor of their success—over their fellow advantaged. If we wish to talk about the sacrifices we should make, given our past offenses against these individuals, this might be one that would make a difference. Furthermore, having made the step of considering the nonmilitary use of the military to effect some redress with regard to these problems, we might also think of using the young people there, not for military purposes as such, but as an organized force of young men and women for redress of our sins against our common environment. They could begin a large-scale assault on the state of our rivers and streams, our cities and our highways. We are told on all sides by them and by those who claim to know their minds that these battles are their hearts' interest. We are affluent enough not to need their labor for other purposes during this period of their lives, but we may not be affluent enough to keep them from these tasks.

are almost always out of hand. The universal practice of training military personnel in camps and other areas where entrance and egress are restricted—a curious fact that that is generally taken for granted—does not eliminate feedback effects from this source. Armed force contexts do provide the maximum possibilities of inculcating high rates of change with a minimum of side effects. Nowhere in the world does it seem probable that armed forces will be eliminated; yet everywhere in the world, with only a few notable exceptions, people claim they wish to keep them in idleness. The solution to conspicuous militarization may be the nonmilitary uses of the military.

6

The Use of Money
and the Distribution
of Income

Uses of Money

Money is a device for effecting an exchange of two or more
things among two or more individuals. Defined that broadly,
money has been characteristic of all peoples. There have
never been any peoples who never exchanged anything for
anything else with anyone else. When we ordinarily think of
the term "money," however, we think of a specific medium
of exchange with some sort of an official backing from the
state, and we think of a medium of exchange that can be
exchanged for a very large number of things. People differ
with regard to the number of things that can be exchanged
in terms of their monies and with regard to how many
monies they recognize. The greater the number of things
that can be exchanged in terms of a given money, the
greater is the "generalization of the medium of exchange."
Most people, even the members of societies of considerable
scale, have been familiar with monies of very limited generalization. In many feudal types of societies, for example,
land could not ordinarily be bought and sold. In our govern-

ment, offices are, ideally speaking, not for sale. We do, however, assume that most of what we regard as the necessities and the luxuries of life will be purchased. The non-modernized have in general relied on purchasing for only a fraction of their needs. This is, of course, closely related to those high levels of self-sufficiency and decentralization mentioned before.

Another of the truly radical features of modernization is that, short of introducing a system of direct allocation, the more highly modernized a society becomes, the greater is the number of things that its members can exchange in terms of money. Highly developed uses of money are very much taken for granted by modernized people. Yet experience along such lines is extremely limited for the non-modernized. Indeed, increased uses of money constitute one of the most spectacular ways of throwing open the horizons of the possible as far as the nonmodernized peoples are concerned.

Most of us, especially academics, are a bit shamefaced about the question of money. The affluent seem to feel that an overt concern with the commodity is indelicate, and the less affluent have other reasons for being diffident about it, but we cannot afford to neglect the subject of money. We are fond of pointing out that reading and travel broaden our perspective. Both reading and travel cultivate our critical faculties for these begin always with a sensitivity to comparisons. Yet for humankind in general it is unlikely that either reading or travel has stimulated critical capacities as much as increased uses of money. For increased uses of money inevitably suggest comparisons and possibilities that have almost certainly never occurred to the individuals concerned before. To point out that the latest volume of pornography costs $2.50 and that a famous Rembrandt has sold for two and a half million dollars is to suggest a comparison—however crass it may seem—between that Rembrandt and that volume. As a minimum one of them is worth a million times as much as the other to somebody. Merely to remark to a nonmodernized person that a higher education costs $1,000 may suggest something quite revolutionary to her or him. It not only conveys the idea of the magnitude of the cost of a higher education; it also conveys the idea that in some sense a higher education can be purchased. A nonmodernized farmer may envisage no possibility whatsoever of getting her or his hands on $1,000 or its equivalent, but by that very remark you have implanted in the farmer's mind the possibility that, should she or he lay hands on $1,000, a higher education with all that might mean for a farmer's daughter, younger sister, son, younger brother, or whomever might be acquired.

Incidentally, cynicism about uses of money is often naive. There can be no lasting human context in which any and everything can be bought if the price is high enough. It is true, however, that for any society the greater the uses of money, the higher is the probability that uses and distribution of money will be closely correlated with prestige and power in other respects. If, however, one could buy any and everything, the correlation would be perfect.*

The general subject of the uses of money and their relation to modernization—for example, the relevance of money as a store of value for capital formation and hence for modernization in general—is more properly treated by technical economists. I have tried to stress here elements connected only with the level of generalization of money. That is one general type of social implication of the sort of uses of money inevitably associated with changes in the direction of modernization. To the extent that this and other facets of the use of money are unperceived or unappreciated, they

* See below, pp. 89–92.

too may constitute one of the factors involved when, for latecomers, things seem suddenly to come apart at the seams without modernization getting very far in any sense acceptable to the people directly involved or to others.

Distribution of Income

We are as queer in our distribution of income as in our use of money. All of the nonmodernized peoples in the history of the world have been characterized by one type of income distribution. That type is illustrated by Figure 3.

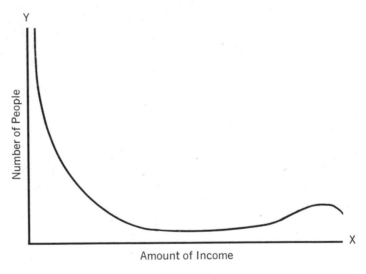

FIGURE 3

The Y axis measures the number of people and the X axis the amount of income. The distribution illustrated is one in which the vast majority of people have very low incomes, indeed; very few people have middling incomes; and a small number of people have very high incomes. It matters little whether one refers to this as exploitation or not; that is the way it has been. Furthermore, just as it is correct to say that a human never lives without regard to bread—even though she or he does not live by bread alone—it is also quite tenable to hold that, while the distribution of income may not determine the distribution of everything else, there are very few things with which we are concerned that vary at random to the distribution of income. The political ideals or preferences of either leaders or people have very little to do with the matter. Today the overwhelming majority of the population of the Peoples' Republic of China have very low incomes or are permitted to spend a very small amount per individual or have a very small amount spent on them. There are comparatively few people to whom middling amounts are allocated, and top political leaders and especially the students receiving higher education have a great deal more spent on them per capita than do others.

Regardless of whether or how wicked such a distribution of income may be judged, it is very difficult to change it. The people of high incomes frequently live wastefully indeed by certain of our values, and are often people of questionable merit by practically anyone's standards. If a fairy godmother, however, were to expropriate their incomes and distribute them peaceably and easily among the vast majority of the people who have very little, the odds are overwhelming that the small additional amount per person would immediately be directly consumed in additional food or the like, and some of the capital formation that keeps the general standards of living as high as they are would thereby be dissipated. In the next year's measurement, income might continue to be as equally distributed as was just achieved, but it would be even lower. If the leaders of the state make up for this by forced savings, some of the income will be differentially expended on different segments of the population, if only because special forms of education are so important a part of capital formation for modernization. No generally acceptable moves toward more equal distributions of income are viable until some process moves the average income to much higher levels.

Modernization may involve many wickednesses, but in the course of the process, this is exactly what does happen. As modernization proceeds, the distribution of income moves in the direction pictured in Figure 4. It is true that in a

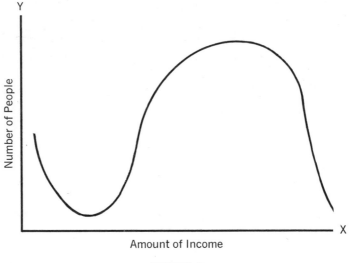

FIGURE 4

country like the United States the improvement of income in the lower income-receiving part of the population lags far behind that of the top 70 percent; in recent years the income of the unemployed and of the unskilled may in fact have lost ground. This is the sort of thing, however, that can be remedied by such a device as the negative income tax. Indeed, one of the things on which practically everyone is agreed is that the present state of the least advantaged 20 to 30 percent of the population is inexcusable. In that judgment there inheres a peculiarly wry tribute to the process. Even without subscribing to the divine American idiocy that holds that there should be no lowest 30 percent of the income distribution, it is certainly possible, if we have the will to do it, to increase radically the portion of income received by the lowest 30 percent. That has never before been true in history, for always before in history that lowest portion of the income distribution amounted to something in excess of 80 percent of the population, so that even equal redistribution of all of the income received by the remaining 20 percent of the population would initially have increased the share of disadvantaged individuals only slightly, and in succeeding periods of income distribution the absolute income of those individuals would have diminished again.

When in highly modernized countries like the United States anyone speaks of power to the people, that may in fact be a statement of the problem: if the speaker means by the "people" something approaching 60 to 70 percent of the population, that is exactly who has the power regardless of how well or how ill they may use it. Never before high levels of modernization has the proportion of the population living close to the margin of subsistence fallen anywhere close to as low a figure as 20 or 30 percent of the population,[1] save possibly in the case of storied benign Pacific Islands and the like. The ineluctable lure of modernization inheres in the material productivity that makes this possible.

[1] To avoid irrelevant argument, I have taken the whole range of the percentages of the members of U.S. society described as living under poverty-stricken conditions as living close to the margin

Furthermore, even under modernized conditions, when the actions of government leaders and the like are able to induce very high levels of forced savings, in the long run the shares of income allocated to an increasing proportion of the population will always increase. There is no sharp turning back from those increases without social upheavals, after which those increases will probably continue again unless the whole system is destroyed. In the long run modernized systems always become geared to the mass acquisition of heavy consumer goods. Once this has been achieved there is apparently no turning back, though there has begun to be a great deal of talk about it.

In our current panic there are those who feel we have made a god of productivity increases and who feel that the situation demands that we give up this religion. This we cannot do no matter how fervently we may wish it; for it would condemn the population of the world permanently to a radically asymmetrical distribution of income or to a redistribution of world income that will not be tolerated or tolerable. The current gross discrepancies in income distribution between the average inhabitant of, say, India and the United States will increasingly become a source of exacerbation. This is not a problem that can be solved simply by expropriating the income of the average citizen of the United States and redistributing it around the world, any more than the problem of the average members of a nonmodernized society could be solved by redistributing the income of the wealthy members of their society. We

---

of subsistence. As margins of subsistence have generally been reckoned elsewhere, it is doubtful that more than 5 percent of our population lives so precariously. Since, however, margins of subsistence, like so many things, can be fruitfully considered to be relative rather than absolute, I have used the larger percentages. The condition alleged is still rare as the experience of humankind goes.

shall not solve our ecological problems by lowering productivity or stagnating it. If we are to solve them at all, we
are going to have to find methods of increasing productivity
in ways that do not threaten survival ecologically. All talk to
the contrary is an ostrich form of breast-beating.

All of this is closely related to the general question of
asceticism. Only three forms of asceticism have ever been
generalized to any mass of any population. Those three are
the asceticism of poverty, the asceticism of true belief, and
the asceticism of striving for mastery over the things of
this world that (thanks to the influence of Professor Max
Weber) we associate with the Protestant Ethic. The last of
these three is probably essential if the patterns of modernization are to persist. There are many who are certainly prepared to question whether this is a good thing. I do not
care to argue the point one way or the other. However
appealing the philosophy of life of the flower children may
be—and it certainly has great appeals along many dimensions—if a fairy godmother were to wave her wand and a
substantial proportion of modernized peoples were vol-
untarily and without coercion to turn to the flower way
of life, the flower Weltanschauung would be the philosophy
of death not life. The material productivity per capita of
flower children is approximately 25 percent of that of a
Vietnamese farmer—it may be less.[2] Given current levels of
population density and interdependence, any substantial return to such levels of productivity in any highly modernized
context would probably result in a death rate not inferior
to that of a nuclear holocaust. The problem of the peoples
of the world is how and whether we can live with modernization at all, not whether we can live without it.

One further observation about the distribution of income
is relevant here. The more highly modernized a society be-

[2] Statistical source: my best guess.

comes, the higher becomes the correlation between income, power, and prestige. In and of itself this should not be surprising. Obviously, there can be no society in which income, power, and prestige vary at random unless there is a society for whose members (1) nothing prestigeful or relevant to power can be gained by the use of income; (2) prestige is in no way used to legitimize power or justify the distribution of income; and (3) no one looks up to the powerful, and the powerful never use power to feather their nests.[3] This is especially unlikely to be the case for modernized societies because, as mentioned above, another characteristic of modernized societies is that the more highly modernized they become, the larger and broader are the number and type of things that can be exchanged in terms of money. This will continue to be the case short of introducing a system of direct allocation of everything. Whether we

---

[3] This has long been known. Our Hobbes said in his *Leviathan:* "And in all places, where men have lived by small Families, to robbe and spoyle one another, has been a Trade, and so farre from being reputed against the Law of Nature, that the greater the spoyles they gained, the greater was their honour . . ." (New York: Everyman's Library, E. P. Dutton & Co., 1914), p. 87.

The relationship between income, power, and prestige gets tighter and more explicit with modernization, and increasingly no one is debarred from playing, but the relationship has never been loose for a society as a whole. There are special cases of anomalies, and partial exceptions to this association. The Brahmins of India may be the largest-scale case of individuals whose prestige was far less connected to power and income than is par for the course of human history. The places of the scholar-intellectual in Jewish communities of Middle and Eastern Europe and in Chinese society are other examples. In general, however, humans have looked up to power and rewarded it, have given power and rewards to those they revered, have taken it for granted that the wealthy would be powerful and respected and that the powerful would demand wealth and respect. With modernization, however, exceptions to this association become more unlikely and the evenness of distribution of all three increases.

like it or not, the more highly modernized a society becomes, the broader will become the uses of money as we know it or its equivalent, until we are all told what we may have and when and where.

The interesting thing about this association between power, prestige, and income is that, as a society becomes more highly modernized, the probability increases that in general an individual will be judged to have high income and/or power because she or he deserves high prestige, rather than that an individual will be judged as deserving high prestige and/or power because she or he has high income. Indeed, in all modernized contexts it is considered a criticism of the system if it can be said that an individual is highly thought of and powerful because she or he is rich or is held negligible and weak because she or he is poor. Although the association of income, power, and prestige is high and gets higher with increases in modernization, it is also true that with increasing modernization it becomes less likely *both* ideally and actually that power and prestige will be dependent functions of income—that individuals will be regarded as powerful and prestigious solely or even primarily *because* their income is high.

Only one factor increases this association between income, power, and prestige more radically than the *increase* of modernization itelf: the attempts to carry the level of explicit social planning of income distribution and other social allocations beyond the level of centralization required by the level of modernization so far achieved. Thus incomes, power, and prestige are probably not as highly associated in the United States, where we are presumed to place so much emphasis on monetary income, as they are in the Soviet Union, for example. In the United States today the Chief Justice of the Supreme Court probably has, both ideally and actually, the highest prestige of any member of the legal fraternity, although there are probably a large number of private practitioners who derive a much higher income from the practice of law than the Chief Justice of the Supreme Court. In the Soviet Union it is hardly imaginable that a person of the highest prestige in the legal fraternity would not receive an income and emoluments higher than someone lower in the hierarchy of prestige. The most cynical of our social critics usually remain docile captives of this sort of snobbery. Other things being equal, we are all likely to assume that the professors with the highest incomes are the best professors, however ill-advised the standards for good may be, and we certainly feel they should be, if there are to be any differentials in academic pay. The very academics who decry academic snobbery are quick to point out that many of us are not as well paid as plumbers, and in that is clearly implicit the idea that we ought to be because we are more valuable. I do not wish to argue the correctness of that point of view—merely to suggest that it is extremely general. As long ago as 1960 in a gathering containing some who regarded themselves as the then New Left of Japan, I was given as an example of the ills of the academic system in particular and the social system in general the fact that custodians of buildings now received more than 25 percent as much (perhaps the figure was 50 percent) as the president of the university. The plaintiff felt that a higher correlation between income and prestige was desirable.

7

Towns and Villages

The relation between townsfolk and countryfolk has been as asymmetrical for the nonmodernized as the distribution of income. There are societies of such small scale in terms of territory covered and numbers of individuals involved that the distinction between towns and villages is of little moment. That has not been the case of societies that we think of in terms of countries or nations or the like. The practices of those who don't know this distinction are not likely to be ones that any substantial proportion of the world's population can emulate.

Wherever towns have been distinguished from smaller settlements, be they called villages or hamlets or whatever, the following two generalizations can be maintained for all the nonmodernized peoples. First, the overwhelming majority of all of the members of the society lived in the rural areas. Never were more than a minority of such peoples town-dwellers, save possibly in the case of the Venetian city-states and the Hanseatic League societies, although these urban centers too had their special relationship with rural peoples. The second feature of all nonmodernized peoples has been that they saw the relationship between the rural and urban areas as a sort of one-way flow in the direction of the urban areas. That flow took many forms, rent, taxes, usury, and profits being the most common. When there were flows in the other direction they were not generally recognized as such. The local rural people took it for granted that that was the way life was. They just assumed it and did not regard it as particularly shocking that some sizable percentage of the crops they tended and of the animals they raised would go to support life in the urban centers. The percentage taken for granted varied enormously. For peoples as a whole it probably never fell a great deal below 20 to 40 percent, and frequently it went much higher. The peoples concerned were habituated to some rate roughly regarded as ethical. Views of the ethics of this differed, of course. In Japan, Tokugawa Iyeyasu, when asked how much grain should be left to the peasants, is reputed to have replied, "Leave them enough so that they can neither live nor die," but the margin was not in fact so precisely approached. Whenever the rate taken as the customary one, whether it be 20 or 40 percent mounted to, say, 40 to 70 percent respectively, what we refer to today as peasant revolts were likely to take place. Such peasant revolts were the least revolutionary of movements. Almost without exception they were aimed at the restoration of the status quo ante, rather than at a change in the system as such. They called for renovation, not revolution. These were not movements against the one-way flow as it was envisaged, but rather against that flow's becoming a torrent.

Some time after the beginning of the twentieth century, especially in the United States setting, a very curious thing took place. Developments that were importantly connected with the urban centers resulted in a continuing increase in the productivity of the land per hectare. Always before in history, increases in the productivity per hectare had been episodic and discontinuous. A new irrigation system would be brought into being and would increase productivity per hectare until the system silted up and ran down. In the United States, however, especially from the 1930's on, this process not only became continuous but seemed to be constantly accelerated. This is the agricultural miracle of modernization, and it has made a mockery out of the use of the term "industrialization" as the general equivalent for modernization. In the United States today we have a comparative advantage in the production of grain rather than in the production of steel. My guess is that some time in the future we will find that this unusual development in world history is at least in part an important consequence of what has generally been referred to as the idiocy of the American farm program. That would be wry. It is certainly the particular American achievement the Russians would most like to imitate. It has shown itself to be exportable. Japan does it; it takes place on Taiwan; to some extent it even takes place in South Vietnam and South Korea.

In many cases of latecomers to the process, the resources available to them would seem to argue that modernization would progress most rapidly with most positive effects for increases in the standard of living if modernization of the urban centers were restricted to those improvements of productivity necessary to service the most rapid possible improvements of productivity per hectare in the rural areas. One of the greatest obstacles to such a policy is the fact that in the past one of the features that distinguished the colonial powers from the colonies was that the colonies furnished primary materials, especially agricultural ones, while the colonial power consumed and converted them. The feeling that such a concentration on agricultural activity will continue to be so construed today is a major obstacle.

What is different about the modernized peoples is that the relationship between the rural and urban areas is no longer a one-way flow. Not only is a situation rapidly achieved in which only a minority of the population live in the rural areas and are needed to carry out production there, but, clearly, things that have a focus in the urban centers, when returned to the rural areas, increase productivity per hectare continuously. Our research laboratories, our industrial plants, our training schools are largely urban, and what is done in them is critical for the productivity of our rural areas. In the past we have been more dazzled by the increase in productivity per worker in the rural area than by the increase in productivity per hectare. It is possible to increase the former without the latter, but it is not usually possible to increase the latter without the former. To increase productivity per worker is quite important from many points of view, but to increase productivity per worker *and* productivity per hectare--especially the latter— that is the most important thing if modernization is to be used to redress the age-old relationship between rural and urban inhabitants—to change that one-way flow. Of course, if major increases in productivity per hectare don't take place, no major redress can be effected. Since the rate of redress, alas, need not be closely tied to those increases, increases in productivity alone will not be enough. New forms of relationships—usually principally via changes in land tenure—must be found so that the changes in productivity can, via increases in income, give hope, motivation, and actual improvement to the 80 percent of the people who are farmers.

It is no accident that so many of the social movements associated with modernization seem to pit rural versus urban peoples. Most of the nonmodernized people have lived very close to the margin of subsistence and, of course, most of them have been rural. If friction is to be avoided over any long run in a modernizing world, three things must be provided for farmers: security of life and existence, a greatly increased probability of general social mobility, and the prospect of particular economic improvement as a result of greatly increased productivity per hectare. With increases in modernization there is absolutely no reason why all three of these things cannot be achieved, although they aren't usually.

8

Education for Modernization

The question of education has been already referred to several times above. The problem of education for an unknown future is sufficiently dramatic and special to justify the special treatment it has been given separately above. There are, however, a number of other special facets of education in the context of modernization that can stand comment. These can be briefly headed as follows: (1) universal education, (2) education in terms of schools, and (3) higher education.

Universal Education

One of the first things that strikes latecomers is the requirement for "universal education." It is only our habit of thinking of education as occurring solely in the specialized contexts of schools (already mentioned above and to be further discussed below) that leads any of us to think that there is something special about this. After all, some forms of education have always taken place for the members of all

known societies. Not only does everyone learn the commonalities of being human insofar as these are not instinctively
determined, but the vast majority learn to sow and to reap,
to cook and to build shelters, and so forth. When we speak
of universal education as one of the characteristics of
highly modernized societies and as one of the special
problems of latecomers to modernization, we mean as a
minimum attaining universal or nearly universal literacy.
Contrary to our general belief, the great change in history
with regard to literacy rates was not a consequence of the
invention of printing. It is true that China and Japan probably had higher literacy rates than any other nonmodernized
peoples, but it is extremely doubtful that literacy rates
exceeded 30 percent of the population concerned either
before or after printing was invented. The discovery of
printing in Europe many centuries later in the fifteenth
century did not lead to anything approaching universal
literacy; indeed, it is extremely doubtful that literacy rates
reached or exceeded 30 percent in European settings until
well into the nineteenth century. Printing has its relevance
no doubt, and I would not wish to slight it, but modernization is a more critical variable in predicting high rates of
literacy. Other things being equal, the more highly modernized a people the higher will be their literacy rates until
in highly modernized societies something approaching universal literacy has been achieved.

We use literacy as a synonym for a whole set of learn-
ings. Learning to write is regarded as the obverse of learning to read, but we also expect a universal literacy with
regard to such fields as arithmetic, and even, oddly enough,
some of the general facts and myths of the history and
civics of the peoples concerned. All of these become part
of the basic—that is, that which they share or expect to
share with the other members of their society—as opposed

99

to the specialized or intermediate learning of modernized people. Other things being equal, the less modernized a people, the less will be the absolute amount of their basic learning, and the less will be the development of their intermediate or specialized learning. With modernization the acceleration of development of specialized learning is so enormously great that we are sometimes bedazzled into ignoring the enormous increase in basic learning. Some realization of this as it applies today is implicit in the joking we do about the "New Math." It is not just a joke. A level of mathematical sophistication extending increasingly to the use of computers is a part of basic learning for our children, though it was not for us.

In considering the enormous increase in basic education, no one can afford to overlook the leveling effect of participation in it. When only the elite learn to read—and perhaps only a small segment of them as in the Middle Ages —literacy is one characteristic by which you can identify the elite. Nowadays you can't tell the Joneses from the Astors *that* way. One of the greatest "democratizing" forces in the history of the world has been the sharing of a common curriculum. Beyond the basic common curriculum of learning to walk and to talk and to eat and to sleep and control bodily functions and interact with other human beings, the common curriculum for all humankind has never been so great as it becomes with modernization. Moreover and especially, never before in history has it exhibited a tendency to become continuously greater all the time. The expansion of basic knowledge is in a sense even more spectacular, though usually ignored, than the proliferation of the specialized knowledge that rests on it. The most spectacular part of all icebergs is the part you never see unless you dive deep.

100

Education in Terms of Schools

It is difficult even to discuss universal education as we think of it without referring directly or indirectly to the use of schools as the device to handle education. For non-modernized people schools, as we think of them, are restricted almost entirely to small portions of the elite. Even for the elite, much of the schooling was provided by individual tutors and the like, rather than by schools as we think of them. Schools represent a special organizational device focused on education. Schools (as already indicated above, pp. 42–51) stand in immediate and stark contrast to one of the great universals of the nonmodernized experience. That universal is that for the nonmodernized the overwhelming proportion of *all* education for all individuals has taken place in family contexts, not just in the first three years or so of life, but throughout the life cycle of the individual. As modernization continues, however, it becomes overwhelmingly likely that the vast majority of all that will be considered education will take place in nonfamily settings known as schools. The break is especially dramatic and traumatic for latecomers who are not yet accustomed, if they are young, to learning things of great importance from people who are not older members of their own families. Furthermore, and no less strategic, the older individuals are not used to having their young learn things of great importance from individuals who are not members of their own families and who are not under their tutelage and control. The overwhelming majority of all of the young, especially of the nonmodernized peoples, spend the vast majority of all of their time, including their learning time, in family contexts or those closely associated with family contexts. With modernization all spend an increasing proportion of their time in schools. What happens to them there is regarded as critical both by them and by others. (Even the most negative critics of our schools regard what happens there as critical even when they hold it not to be "relevant" or perhaps because they hold it not to be "relevant.")

The general exposure of any substantial proportion of the population to education in terms of schools is something that no peoples have experienced much longer than a hundred years. Probably most of the world's population has not had much experience with it for as much as half a century. As long as families, or some closely related organizational contexts such as neighborhood groups, clans, and so forth, are the ones in terms of which most people do most things most of the time, the fact that learning takes place there simply reinforces the general relevance of such settings. To the extent that schools replace a part of that, some of the relevance of such contexts is destroyed, but it cannot be automatically replaced by the school context. For the vast majority of people the family context is, after all, a continuing one. Even in our own lives where we string schooling out much longer than anyone else has done in history, the schools are, for practically everybody, specifically a transitional context—a training or preparatory context. A school is not a general living context except for those in the process of training. This may be one of the reasons why people who remain perpetually in school contexts, as do university faculties, have from many points of view a childish aura about them. It may also explain why life in school at any level—even when the great majority of all those of appropriate age experience it— is somehow still generally regarded as something apart from the "real world."

Higher Education

Today we not only take universal education for granted and education in terms of schools for granted; we also take higher education for granted. The United States is the first set of peoples for whom a college education has become, in the literal sense of the term, vulgar. Some years ago, in 1965, something in excess of 70 percent of our children completed secondary school and better than 55 percent of those went on to some form of higher education. We must already have reached a situation in which something in excess of 40 percent (perhaps in excess of 50 percent by the time this book is published) of all of the children born to us go on to some form of higher education. There are practically none among us who do not expect and want that percentage to increase. As has been true of a secondary school education before, a college education is sure to become a part of the basic education of our people. The Japanese will probably be the second people to do this, and the clamor of others is already being heard. Such advanced schooling is not compatible with high rates of productivity in other respects on the part of the students during their school years. Unless we find a different way of combining activities with schooling, we shall continue to have to live with the fact that only extremely affluent societies can afford to keep any substantial proportion of their young out of other productive pursuits for their first twenty to twenty-two years of life. To put it another way, only the members of highly affluent societies can make higher education universal.

Like the other factors having to do with education mentioned above, the tendency toward more widespread higher education is also exported in advance of other elements of modernization to latecomers to the processes. I have already indicated that inadvertently we export our academic snobbery in these respects to these people as well (see note 1, pp. 48–49). We also export other things. We guarantee that for a long time after modernization begins we will importantly pye the civil service attempts of the latecomers by our generally unexamined assumption that the proper training for any role in governance is a college education. It is one thing to make that assumption when the vast majority of all of the young people who are likely to go into government at all can be expected to have college educations. It is quite another thing to export that idea when only a small minority of the youth of a country can hope to achieve college educations and where the caliber of those college educations may also leave a great deal to be desired. We jest to the effect that the graduates of our elite colleges and graduate schools are well suited to be special advisors to the secretary of state or the like, but that is to poke fun at the pretensions of our elite colleges and universities.

In most nonmodernized settings even to have aspired to higher education may be a mark of distinction. In a setting in which it is a matter of pride to point out that one has failed the entrance examinations to Cambridge, those who have had any experience of higher education are, *indeed,* too elite to accept positions which, though beneath their elite distinction, are well beyond them in experience. To place them in the kind of bureaucratic positions justified by academic snobbery is to place them in positions for which they are ill-prepared and hence it guarantees troubles for the bureaucracy. To refuse them such positions is to guarantee a highly disgruntled and articulate elite.

In this respect the experience of armed forces contexts is highly apposite. After all, armed forces, when they are not afighting, are essentially training and educational contexts. An enormous number of armed forces in history have hit upon the following device. Given the best recruits attainable, whether by universal conscription or by voluntary procedures, those who show aptitude as privates are sent to corporal schools (or special courses); if they succeed at corporal schools, they are made corporals; if they are good corporals, they are sent to sergeant schools; if they are good at sergeant schools, they are made sergeants; and so on until, following Peter's Principle, they have been promoted to the level of their incompetence. What that does—without anybody's having thought it out very well—is to adjust the level and nature of advanced training to the level of relevant experience insofar as that can be determined. There is absolutely no reason why this cannot be done in nonmilitary contexts. Given the values and requirements of most of the latecomers, college degrees should not be regarded even as an initial ideal in civilian governmental contexts. Young people who have the required basic education in literacy could be taken in and sent along for further schooling as their experience and achievements warrant. That would be one way of getting a closer relationship between experience and relevant higher education than is presently obtainable. I suspect that a major obstacle to doing this may very well be that the military do it and therefore it is autonomically considered inalienably military and hence improper for civilian contexts.

There is another factor having to do with higher education that is of some importance. Universities are curious organizations with a long history. In general, only three things have ever been done well in university contexts (and the members of most universities have probably not succeeded in doing those three very well). Those three things are the preservation of knowledge, the transmission of knowledge, and the discovery of new knowledge.[1] The service of universities to the larger community must, if the universities are to be viable, consist primarily of performances along some combination of these three lines.

For a good number of years most of us have been cynical about how good a job is done in terms of the transmission of knowledge. No major proportion of the general public has ever been terribly interested in the preservation of knowledge. So in recent times perhaps the most striking feature of universities has been their contributions to the discovery of new knowledge. This is in and of itself a special development. Throughout most of their histories universities have been primarily important for their contributions to the preservation and transmission of knowledge. As the modernization process developed, two curious things took place. On the one hand, continual increases of basic and specialized knowledge became increasingly critical for survival, let alone the good life, and, on the other hand, the overwhelming organizational focus for the discovery of new knowledge came to be the university or a university-simulated organization. Prior to the twentieth century, the universities were not the main settings through which contributions to knowledge were developed.

By a series of historical accidents the United States has become the overwhelming repository of world university resources, especially with regard to contributions to knowledge at the frontiers of discovery. Universities are delicately poised and curiously tolerated organizations. For a whole series of reasons the temptations for latecomers to develop them quickly, and for the modernized as well as the non-modernized to attempt to use universities for purposes other

[1] Especially in recent U.S. history, participant recreation for the young and vicarious recreation for their elders may add a fourth category of things well done in university settings.

than the three mentioned above—especially to use them as primarily political devices—are certain to be very great, indeed, both from within and from without the university. Such attempts will never accomplish the purposes they are intended to serve over any extended period, but they may easily result in the destruction of the universities. If that happens generally in the modernized world, we shall have to look to other contexts for the discovery of needed new knowledge, just as those peoples who have not developed universities must do now.

9

Recreation and Politics

There are no peoples who have not had some specialized forms of recreation. There are no peoples who know no games. For most of the people most of the time, however, their recreation has been an aspect of other things they did. The distinction between "working" and "living" that the highly modernized take for granted does not come easily to the nonmodernized. The most highly modernized people have a special problem in this respect, since they are in the throes of what one might call the leisure revolution. With a forty-hour work week plus suitable vacations, let alone what a thirty-five or thirty-hour work week would imply, we are already faced with a peculiar problem for humankind. How do you keep people happy and well-adjusted when they are not busy keeping body and soul together, when the time that they must work to live occupies only a minority of their waking hours? The vast majority of the nonmodernized people have not had any such amount of leisure time, and in addition they have lived on the bare margin of subsistence. We, on the other hand, not only have such time but live on a very affluent level, indeed—for all of the disgraceful condition of the lowest 20 or 30 percent of our income receivers.

One of the most ironic problems of highly modernized

people is how to adjust to and live with the kind of leisure combined with affluence that most humans have not yet found within their horizons of the possible. Recreation whether by direct participation or vicarious participation in spectator sports and the like is a vital element in this. Having conquered the problem of bread, the provision of circuses may be even more important for us.

In some sense the latecomers receive precocious experience of the role of recreation for the highly modernized, but there is one special form of recreation in which they participate long before modernized levels of achieved affluence and acquired leisure time characterize them. That special form has to do with the recreational aspects of politics— politics as recreation, you might say.

Whether the political procedures of latecomers will be properly described as "democratic" is highly questionable, but there is no question that in the political procedures of both latecomers and the highly modernized there will be mass participation in what are generally called political activities. That participation may be highly permissive in some cases, but in most cases it is likely to be highly organized or regimented either by explicit bureaucratic organization or by devotion to charismatic leaders—or by both. The vast increases in efficiency and utilization of communication devices guarantee an almost overnight increase in awareness of people even in the remote areas of the countries concerned —an awareness that never characterized these people before. Furthermore, whatever the political processes have been in the past, unless the societies concerned are very small-scale societies indeed, the probability of there having been mass participation at any save the most discrete local levels is extremely small.

There is an undeniably heady aspect about direct general participation in the "political process." In the United

States we have become rather blasé about this. We have an unusually long history of direct participation at least by a considerable proportion of the male population. You might say that we have shifted from politics as recreation to recreation as politics. In the nineteenth century the recreational aspect of political participation was inescapable. The long political debates of that period were an important recreational form, though we can hardly credit it today.[1] We do see brief recrudescences of this, for example, the first time our political conventions were televised, the Nixon-Kennedy debates, and so forth. On the whole we are more likely to turn our recreational events into political events (for example, the Woodstock affair) than find much entertainment value in the political processes as such. Even here, however, we still see important remnants of it. The recreational aspects of political participation as viewed on university campuses is inescapable among us.

For latecomers to modernization the recreational overtones of political participation are also inescapable. The freedom chanters of Africa, the "demos" of Japan (the Japanese even describe their different formations as different types of dances), the Red Guards—one cannot see films or witness these events without being struck by the fact that the participants in some critical respects are enjoying themselves. This crops up again in grimmer contexts. The riots in our ghettos, the religious fighting in India, and mob actions in general all involve many people for whom participation is an act of fierce enjoyment, however short-lived it may be for some of them. Despite all our humanistic hopes, there is a major recreational exhilaration in violence for many of

[1] A large audience sitting through a political speech of two or more hours is a mark par excellence of dictatorship for us today, though this was certainly not the case for our foremothers and forefathers at the time of the Douglas-Lincoln debates.

us—perhaps for all of us. Given the conditions under which some of us live all of the time and all of us live some of the time, no one has yet succeeded in taking the fun out of murder, rapine, pillage, and arson.

There is nothing new about the recreational aspects of mass participation in anything. The thing that is new with modernization is that mass participation in one way or another in the political process is par for the course. The recreational appeal of political processes becomes a critical variable—precociously for latecomers—since for them mass participation, whether democratic or no, will begin ever earlier and more intensely if only because of our improvements in the technology of communication. In such situations the alternative to given political appeals may as well be recreational appeals as other political appeals. In nonmodernized areas it is probably easier to divert the young from a given political allegiance by free driving lessons than by attempts at political conversion. For us bread and circuses take on new relevance.

10

A Sexual Revolution

It is difficult to write about sex and modernization without running the risk of either, on the one hand, a pretension—in my case—to a lurid type of virtuosity and experience or, on the other, the wrath of the put-upon ladies of our time. Nevertheless, it is an important subject. In the sexual revolution discussed here—and it is only one of the sexual revolutions and not the one generally discussed today—one of the most radical changes in the entire history of humankind has taken place under our very noses with practically none of us having been aware of it at all. Even those writers who have touched on the subject in one way or another have not in general been aware of how radical a change they touched.

In all known societies—in all the aggregations of human-kind of which we have any knowledge whatsoever—the young have had their most intensive learning experiences in a family setting from the beginning of their lives. Whatever words have been used to teach them, they have initially learned everything about who they were and who others were in terms of three distinctions: age, generation, and sex. The sociology of this is something of a bore. Initially, all infants have learned, for example, that they were followers because they were infants or children, because they represent a younger generation, and because they were, perhaps, female. They did not learn that they were female, of a younger generation, and infants because they were followers. Mind, I pass no judgment on the worth of this; I simply assert it as an hypothesis about a universal fact.

Of these three categories in terms of which all human beings seem to have learned their places in the world, one —the category of sex—is peculiar. The distinctions applied of age and generation are basic to *all* members of the society. The sex distinction is the first learned *specialized* or intermediate distinction for all humans. It is the first experience human beings have of a characteristic that we share with some, but never share with others. After all, all of us were or are in some sense infants. And all of us in some sense are or were representatives of a younger generation. All of us become children and become representatives of older generations if we survive long enough. *But* in all known social settings of the world in which human beings have existed at all, from birth roughly 50 percent have been little males and the other 50 percent little females. They have always been treated differently from one another and made to realize at extremely early stages that they were different. Furthermore, as nearly as we can make out, the difference in treatment is always carried much further than we are presently able to account for on purely physiological grounds.

It will be amusing if this turns out to be merely a cultural trick on the part of a bunch of dirty-minded old men. If that turns out to be the case—if one can assume, as some seem to today, that it was left to men to hit upon it and women to accept it—we shall have a further interesting problem because that is the one invention that all men seem to have hit upon, and almost all women seem to have to some degree accepted throughout time. Since, quite apart from the grosser anatomical differences between males and females, every cell in the male body is different in structure

113

from every cell in the female body, by virtue of its chromosomal structure, if nothing else, nothing would seem to be simpler than the hypothesis that those differences do have implications for the ways in which people behave, and that some of these, however bizarre they may seem and however inegalitarian they may be, may very well have had survival value.

Again, it is not meet to pass judgment on this here. After all, survival is by no means everything, and we do not even know for certain that this distinction has had survival value—just that some form of it is universal. To assume that what is universal is either good, or specifically selected for in an evolutionary sense, is vulgar teleology, pure and simple. Regardless of whether distinction among individuals on the basis of their sex is fair or good, and regardless of whether the distinctions that have been made bear any close resemblance to those necessary for survival or are implicit in the minimal physiological distinctions among the biological individuals—one fact is certain: all human beings of whom we have any knowledge have been so differentiated from birth. It is the first form of specialized treatment—of treatment that one set of individuals receive and others do not—that all individuals have in some sense experienced. Initial treatments of infants on the basis of age and generation are basic differentiations; initial treatment of infants on the basis of sex is a specialized or intermediate differentiation. If what I have asserted as fact is so, then, I believe it must follow that subsequent human learning about specialization is in some sense heaped on the shoulders of learning to distinguish the sexes, and to be so distinguished.

I have gone into the matter at such length because the modernization process has not been "idle" in this matter of sex. One of the most revolutionary things about modernization is a characteristic that has accompanied the process in this realm. In all known societies, including our own, the overwhelming majority of individuals in the steepest part of their learning curves have been reared largely in a family setting—and regardless of whether they were little males or little females—have been reared largely under the direct supervision and care of their mothers and other female members of the family or other females closely associated with the family members. For most of the history of the world the relevance to this of a suitable supply of food for infants is too obvious to require discussion.[1]

For those who survived, an interesting thing took place as the little children grew older, say, at approximately four or five years of age. For a good part of the day the little boys went off—usually to the fields—with their fathers and older brothers, if they had them. If they went to long houses or club organizations or the like, in any case they went with males, and some of those males were older males. The little girls continued under the direct domination and supervision of women even when they went to similar places. Regardless of the kind of contacts the little boys and girls may have had during other parts of the day, during that part of the day in which they learned the sort of thing that we associate with schooling of the young today, they learned

---

[1] I believe some Bavarians in the seventeenth century seem to have generally bottle fed, or by some other method fed, their infants, but their demography and other characteristics were quite unusual. See J. Knodel and E. Van de Walle, "Breast Feeding, Fertility and Infant Mortality: An Analysis of Some Early German Data," *Population Studies* 21, no. 2 (September 1967): 109–131; J. Knodel, "Infant Mortality and Fertility in Three Bavarian Villages: An Analysis of Family Histories from the 19th Century," *Population Studies* 22, no. 3 (November 1968): 297–318; and J. Knodel. "Two and a Half Centuries of Demographic History in a Bavarian Village," *Population Studies* 24, no. 3 (November 1970): 353–376.

it on a sexually segregated basis—not coeducationally—at least they learned a very large part of it that way. Again, I am not interested in passing any judgment on this. I only point to the fact that in terms of world history, coeducation, as we take it for granted, is bizarre and exotic—and, as a general phenomenon, recent.

It was usually from older members of their own families that they learned these things on a sexually segregated basis, but the essence of the matter is not that they were members of their own families but that from roughly age five to maturity at, say, age fifteen, the little males for a good part of their daily existence were under the direct domination and supervision of older males, and the little females continued under the direct domination and supervision of older females. At roughly age fifteen—sometimes a bit earlier and sometimes a bit later—they were considered to be mature.

A funny thing happened in the United States on the way into the twentieth century. The overwhelming majority of males came to have jobs where they could not take the little boys along with them even if they wished to do so. In the United States, though not equally in other modernized countries, this happened at roughly the point in time at which the great organizational context that took up children's time other than the family—the schools—came to be manned largely by ladies, except possibly for the top positions such as those of principal. As a result, for the first time in the history of humankind, the overwhelming majority both of little boys and of little girls continued under the direct domination and supervision of ladies until they reached maturity. This has never happened before in history. Crusades, war, migrations, pestilence—nothing for a people as a whole ever before took so large a percentage of young adult and older adult males out of family contexts for so much of the waking time of children. When we discuss the problems of the young and speak of generation gaps today in highly modernized contexts, we are talking about an unusual set of people.

Our young are the first people of whom the following can be said: if they are males, they and their fathers and their brothers and sons and all the males they know are overwhelmingly likely to have been reared under the direct domination and supervision of females from birth to maturity. No less important is the fact that their mothers and their sisters and their girl friends and their wives and all of the ladies with whom they have to do have had to do only with males so reared. Most of us have not even noticed this change, nor do we have any realization of its radicality. We certainly do not have any systematic body of speculation on what the significances of so radical a change are or could be. To put the matter as dramatically as possible, we do not even know whether viable human beings can over any long period of time be reared in such a fashion. After all, this has never held true of any substantial proportion of any population for even one generation in the history of the world until the last fifty years. This has not held true for two generations, for any substantial portion of any population for more than twenty years at the outside. It has not yet characterized any substantial portion of any population for three generations, but most of those living today will live to see what this will be like!

This is a very different kind of matrifocality than the presumed matrifocality of the ghetto. The matrifocality of the ghetto is a matrifocality by default. It results from family disruption usually as a result of desertion by or episodic replacement of a male family head. The kind of matrifocality alleged here is quite compatible with stable male presence and stable male headship of the family. Its effects may be the greater for all that and very far-reaching, indeed. It may account for the fact that most of us like to assume that the creativity of the average individual would be practically unlimited were it not inhibited by ignorant, if not criminal, school practices and other shortcomings of our life, times, and system. It might, on the other hand, also be related to high levels of alienation, crimes of violence—heaven knows what. Most of us are unaware of how radical a change we have undergone, let alone where it leads.

Whatever it is related to, it is an extremely general phenomenon. Of course, the primary and secondary school students of modernized and modernizing societies need not be taught overwhelmingly by ladies as they have in the United States. But the extension of female influence on male offspring past infancy and early childhood to maturity in most family contexts takes place in all highly modernized contexts about which we know anything, and it also takes place in the context of all latecomers. Like the education for an unknown future that is another of the constantly increasing elements in the generation gap,[2] this element of

[2] The "generation gap," so often discussed today, has three elements. First, there is the universal and constant generation gap that is a consequence of the fact that the human organism takes roughly fifteen years to become adult. This gap may vary by a few years from one society to another, but it is the same between father and son as between father and grandfather and similarly for the ladies. When one speaks of the generation gap being always with us, this is the one. This is the one that Plato, Aristotle, and Montaigne wrote about—that Shakespeare wrote about better than anyone else, as he seems to have done about everything held in common by humans. Second, there is the generation gap that results from the fact that the problems of educating children for an unknown future have become endemic. This gap is greater between father and son than between father and grandfather (and similarly for the ladies) and gets greater as modernization continues. Third, there is the generation gap that results from this bizarre matrifocality. Before attributing the generation gap to any quantum increases in the intelligence or moral character of my children by contrast with my own, I would like to know how much of our differences I can

the modernization process is exported precociously to late-comers—again without any design on either our part or theirs.

It is exported in at least two ways. Without thinking about what we are doing to them or they are doing to themselves, new jobs in latecomer settings are overwhelmingly likely to be set up on a basis such that the men cannot take the boys along with them. They can explicitly be set up on that basis, or they can acquire that character simply by people's assuming that the men will not bring the boys along with them.

There is another way in which this takes place, however. For a whole set of reasons there occurs among all latecomers a drift of population to the urban centers. That drift of population is likely overnight to create sex ratios in the urban centers of two to one, or even three to one, males to females. It is the young males who come first to the cities and towns. But like all peoples before them, the sex ratio in the countryside, where 80 percent of the population as a minimum lives, is roughly one to one. As a disproportionate number of males leave the countryside and go to the city, in the rural areas there is a resultant disproportion of females to males, unless someone has done something beastly like kill off an appropriate number of females or suddenly create a disproportionate birth of males or survival rate of males. In both highly modernized contexts and in the context of latecomers this shift—surely one of the most radical social changes in social history—has been a change by default as it were. No one seems to have intended it; no one seems even to have thought much about it.

This sexual revolution has come on little cat's feet. So far

---

explain in terms of these three elements of which the last two are radical new additions to history.

no high levels of violence have been directly associated with this revolution, though we certainly don't know that these changes have nothing to do with the increasing levels of violence that seem to characterize both the highly modernized and latecomers to modernization as well. If the change to which I point has taken place on anything like the scale that I allege, nothing is less likely than that it makes no difference or very little difference.

11

Relationship Aspects

It makes a difference how people relate to one another. Most relationships for nonmodern people have emphasized six elements:

1. Doing things in a given way because that's the way they have been done from time immemorial—doing things for traditional reasons. "We have always plowed this way."

2. Selecting people on the basis of *who* they are—and it was overwhelmingly probable that the basis for determining *who* they are would be a kinship basis of some sort. "My brother will be my minister."

3. Construing the matters covered by the relationship very broadly, subject to all sorts of additional demands by any party to the relationship. "How could I refuse you, Mother?"

4. Dealing with others in a close intimate fashion or on a reserved basis. (Relationships in nonmodernized as in modernized societies vary enormously in this respect.) "I want to know how you feel about it," or "Never mind whether you love me; it is only necessary that you respect me."

5. Requiring all parties to the relationship to be responsible—to have a care for whether the other parties to the relationship got what they sought from it. "I know I do not have to watch you like a hawk."

6. Finally, practically all relationships were hierarchical. Indeed, only one relationship was ideally egalitarian generally and that—friendship—was often hierarchical in actuality. Relationships that were nonhierarchical by virtue of the fact that they were fleeting casual contacts were virtually unknown. The friendship relationships that were egalitarian by ideal were terribly important to given individuals, of course, but no organizational context that was expected to last was importantly based on friendships. (See above, pp. 70–71).

As modernization increases, there is an enormous increase in relationships that emphasize:

1. Doing things for reasons that are rationally justified. "I can prove that this plowing technique gives a higher yield per hectare."
2. Selecting people on the basis of what they can do that is relevant and not barring or preferring them on the basis of who they are. "I don't care who they are as long as they can do the job."
3. Specifically defining and delimiting obligations. "That's all it says on your guarantee."
4. Not becoming personally involved with the other party to the relationship. "Let's keep personal feelings out of this."

Under some circumstances in the modernization process there may be a great increase in relationships that count on each individual's protecting her or his own interests. However, I believe that in the long run with modernization, it can be shown that both ideally and actually there must be a constant increase in the level of responsibility that one takes for one's relationships with others. As in the case of all the nonmodern peoples, the vast majority of these new relationships that develop are hierarchical, but a new category of nonhierarchical relationships is introduced. For highly modern people there is an enormous number of relationships that are nonhierarchical by default, as it were. They are nonhierarchical because they are fleeting casual relationships in terms of which relative rankings are of little or no moment. (These are the relationships discussed above in Chapter 3—our strange relationships with strangers.)

It is important to note that the relationship emphases characteristic of nonmodern peoples are *not at all* eliminated by the modernization process in two important respects. In the first place the relationships emphasizing the second set of qualities mentioned above—rationality, objective recruitment, limited liability, and avoidance—do not replace many of the relationships that previously existed and continue to exist for all peoples. For example, family and kinship relationships continue to follow their old patterns in these respects at least, and every individual's life chances under modern as well as nonmodern conditions are importantly conditioned by those experiences. By far the majority of relationships with the new emphases are newly created relationships altogether. These do not involve a direct conversion of the old. There are new types of jobs, new types of organizational contexts in terms of which one operates, and so forth. Insofar as the old emphases are "reduced," it is largely by such new relationships supplementing and limiting the sphere of operation of the old.

The second respect in which these ancient emphases persist has to do with a peculiar sort of instability that is characteristic of the new emphases, or this special set of emphases, that is not characteristic of the first. If a relationship emphasizes rationality, objective recruitment, limited liability, and avoidance, the longer any given instance of that relationship continues, the greater is the probability that, regardless of what the relationship is like ideally, actually traditional, personal, broadly construed, and intimate patterns will replace the others. Other things being equal, the longer you know someone, the more difficult it is to deal with that person impersonally. The new type emphases, therefore, tend to break down into the old familiar types. When the old familiar types break down, they do not break down in the new direction ordinarily. You do not tend to substitute limited liability relationships for broadly construed ones, but rather alternative broadly construed ones. You switch from a sanctioned intimacy to an unsanctioned one—not to avoidance. If you are supposed to select your relatives for a job, you do not ordinarily deviate by selecting people impersonally but rather by substituting other personal criteria. You switch from one traditional justification to another, not ordinarily from a traditional justification to a rational justification.

One of the reasons why the process of modernization is so disruptive to latecomers is that a large number of new relationship emphases are introduced into the old social context. Thousands of new relationships are generated as levels of interaction rise, and organizations proliferate. The change is less of a wrench than it might otherwise be because this introduction is largely by virtue of the fact that totally new relationships are created, rather than by the conversion of old existing ones. Those old ones are more eroded and diminished by a loss of function—a loss of relevance—than by direct onslaught. There is, however, one major sphere of human behavior in which the new introductions are likely to require direct conversion of the existing patterns. That is in the sphere of government. Most of the governments of nonmodern peoples are based overwhelmingly on the kind of relationship emphases generally characteristic of those people. If any shifts in the direction of modernization are to take place, some attempts must be made to convert those relationships into the other types of emphases. In the new governmental contexts lip service at least must be given to emphases on rationality, merit and achievement, specific and detailed powers and responsibilities, and impersonality. These new emphases are no more stable in government than elsewhere. In this respect at least there is a built-in revolutionary element as far as governments are concerned—quite apart from the myriad other factors with implications for such radical change.

One of the special questions raised for both latecomers to modernization and the highly modernized has to do with the kinds of instability implicit in these new type relationship emphases. One of these types of instability has already been mentioned above. However strongly accepted and affirmed these new emphases may be, the longer a given relationship continues, the greater is the probability that these emphases on rationality, and so forth, will break down in the "unacceptable" alternative direction. There is, however, another problem about stability here. Cases of these new emphases in the past have not been lacking.[1] What is special about these emphases is not that they are in fact new, but that the proliferation of relationships with very high levels of emphases on these qualities is on so large a scale. Indeed, the scale has been so large that whole schools of social scientists speak of these emphases as though they have completely replaced the others, but that, of course, is nonsense.

This second sort of instability seems to me to inhere in the fact that humankind may very well be considerably less well adapted to, and much more ill at ease when trying

---

[1] The Imperial Chinese examination system and the Imperial Chinese bureaucracy are perhaps the most famous precocious example.

to maintain, high emphases on rationality, impersonal selection, carefully defined and delimited relationships, and
avoidance. We speak with some discomfort of individuals'
losing their sense of identity. We refer constantly to cogs
on a wheel, and in general we fail to be aware of the fact
that one respect in which the family has, perhaps, become
more important for modern man is that it is the one organizational environment that can be described as the
"castle of the me."[2] For the generality of highly modernized
people, only the family furnishes a context in which one
can count on being considered as a "whole person." The
high rates of mental illness and the like associated with
high levels of modernization may simply be a function of
improved diagnosis, but they may also be related to such
strains as these.

[2] See above, p. 61.

12

Demographic Changes

Demography—the study and analysis of population usually via statistics—is much too important to be wasted on demographers. Due to the very substantial intellectual advances of our demographers, the utility of demography is very high, indeed. Other things being equal, we are far less likely to fall into errors and misunderstandings crossing a difficult language barrier by asking how many people were born, how many died, how old they were when they died, how many belong to a single family, and so forth, than by asking individuals what their attitudes toward political leadership are, and the like. Most of the things we are interested in may very well not follow directly from the number of people present, their age distribution, their sex distribution, and their mortality rates, but very few of the things in which we are interested can vary at random to these factors. We might be better off trying to test our hypotheses by relating them to demographic factors than by most other means.

In any case some of the demography associated in some sense with modernization has become part of the common sense of our time. The vast majority of all nonmodernized people lived on the margin of demographic subsistence. They were characterized by very short life expectancies.

The ratio of males to females was roughly one to one. They had very high mortality rates, especially high infant mortality rates. The vast majority of all people who survived past puberty got married. The females, once they reached childbearing age, were usually either pregnant or nursing infants or both. Their fertility rates were extremely high—close to the limits of biological possibility. Their rates of population increase were extremely modest. Their populations doubled at very slow rates. Their high fertility barely kept them ahead of their mortality. In many cases in history it must have failed to keep them ahead. Barren marriages were a threat to all.

With modernization there have been several basic changes in this picture. For latecomers, especially, the probability of a rapid change in the mortality figure is overwhelming. Throughout history people have been characterized by high mortality rates, especially high infant mortality rates, but it appears that no one has cared much for them. One of the material elements of modernization that diffuses most easily to the nonmodernized rests on those implications of modern medical technology that save lives or improve the health of the general population. It has become part of the common sense of the modernization question that it is much more difficult to lower the fertility rates than to lower the mortality rates—that the resultant discrepancies create the population flood that threatens to drown us all in fertility.

There are other changes that are less frequently commented upon. Modern medical technology saves not only numerous easily numbered infant lives; it also preserves life at the opposite end of the age scale as well. As life expectancy for the individual approaches seventy—and long before it gets there—latecomers to modernization are faced with a new phenomenon. In most nonmodernized contexts an enormous value has been placed on the aged, but very

128

few individuals have survived long enough to become aged. We still have overtones of that jest when some virtuoso of old age points out, as Casey Stengel did on his eightieth birthday, that "very few people my age are still alive." I suspect that the reason some of the large-scale and exotically developed family organizations could be maintained as ideals is that very few people achieved them. The average size of family units has not in fact varied much through history, despite variations in family ideals.[1]

For people who continue to prefer large families, the change in the demographic situation makes it possible for them, for the first time in their history, to approximate the ideals they have always proclaimed. There is probably no greater stimulus to the development of the small nuclear family that is everywhere characteristic of the highly modernized peoples. To put it bluntly, the fact that under the new demographic dispensations many peoples can have the families they have always said they wanted may very well be the source of the most radical change in what families they want.

There is another kind of implication. For virtually all nonmodernized peoples the family has been *the* form of social insurance for the aged. It is the almost universal expectation that the aged, when they persist, will be taken care of by the younger generation in the context of their own families. In actuality very few individuals survived long past the birth of their first grandchildren. One of the problems of dealing with the aged, quite apart from the fact that they may no longer be productive in a setting in which most people live on the mere margin of subsistence,

---

[1] People who preferred the very largest families, like the Chinese, had families that on the average were considerably less than twice as large as the families of those people who preferred the smallest families.

is that the older they grow, the greater is the probability that they will live long enough to experience senility. Senility is an exceedingly difficult thing to deal with for a whole series of reasons, not the least of which is the episodic nature of disruptive acts of senility and the special hopelessness that goes with the childishness of the aged by contrast with the childishness of the young. Throughout history, however, very few people have lived long enough to become senile, and very few have lived long enough to place a major strain on the family as a form of old age insurance. With the advent of modernization, it is increasingly much better than an even money bet that the vast proportion of all individuals will survive to the point at which old age insurance becomes important. In no highly modernized society is the problem of old age insurance taken care of in an extended family context, and in the United States special residential developments for the care of the aged have become a major form of capital formation.

The miracles of modern medical technology, however, have not yet achieved immortality or the avoidance of senility. While we see about us an increasing number of adepts at old age such as Winston Churchill, we have more than hints that even these become senile. Many of the miracles of modern medical technology can also be exported well in advance of other elements of modernization; indeed, because of the common sentimentality about the preservation of human life, that is exactly what is likely to take place. We may very well see a dramatic case of the implications of this in an extreme form in China (as indicated above, pp. 46–47).

There is another specifically demographic consideration. The enormous increases in population that have resulted from applications of some modern medical technology even when other elements of modernization are highly recalcitrant, given general limitations on space, are radical increases in population density. Even if everything else remained constant, those increases in density would themselves constitute important increases in interdependence. Most of the firstcomers to modernization started the process with relatively low population densities—certainly low by present standards. Many or most of the latecomers begin the process with quite high population densities, which increase more rapidly than other characteristics associated with modernization and more rapidly than before for those latecomers. We can decrease the mortality rates of latecomers faster and more easily than we can build new modern forms of productivity generally; and we can lower mortality rates faster for latecomers than we could for firstcomers.

The old high densities of latecomers were accompanied by high levels of decentralization and by local self-sufficiency such as it was. Their modern situations have a double-dip of increased interdependency—their population explosions and their increasing involvement with modernization. For them the old methods of handling high density problems no longer work, and we find their problems the more difficult to understand because we did not march along these curves with populations already bursting at the seams. Nevertheless, as modernization moves further along, unless we lick human fertility, we and they will come to the same problem: living with the increased interdependence of increased population densities compounded by wildly increasing interdependencies from other sources as well. I suppose the effect has something of the nature of continually increasing the temperature of a gas contained in a cylinder of decreasing size. The strength of the container is not likely to approach infinity.

PART III

The Future and Its Prospects

FOR reasons that escape me it is fashionable for social scientists to discuss the future of modernized societies in terms of thirdhand extrapolations of current technologies. Only our science fiction writers have cut themselves free, as it were, for speculation, and in recent years even these have had their imaginations rather overawed by the extent to which they are acclaimed as prescient. Such speculation as most of us have carried out anent social futures has been extrapolations of our desires and our romances, rather than speculation about probabilities, or at least questions raised by things as they presently seem to be. Fortunately, I suppose, we never know who is really Cassandra until the passage of time has made that knowledge only a basis for bemoaning our insensitivities. I cannot see any basis for the predictions of the year 2000 and the like that somehow seem to hold prospects for increased democracy, unfettered decentralized freedoms, the effortless life devoted to the kind of personal cultivation that the pundit economists, physicists, and sociologists of our world claim to advise in their strikes for attention and/or power. I do agree with our seers on one prediction. Life is not likely to be solitary, poor, nasty, brutish, and short. It may, however, very well be crowded, affluent, nasty, brutish, and long—well, maybe not affluent.

There is an academic voice in the land now. It chants a

mindless optimism about the future—a litany of benign witches whose bell, book, and candle are summed in the phrase, "Post Industrial State." That phrase—only acronymically apt—is their basic answer to despair. Our present problems of want, envy, maldistribution, ceaseless striving, timing, lack of humanism, even bigotry, these say, will be eliminated in the Post Industrial State. But the argument seems to feed on its own tail. We are not told why the Post Industrial State solves our problems—just that it will. You begin to suspect that it solves our problems by definition in two ways: the Post Industrial State is a state that does not have our problems; our problems are problems we won't have when we have the Post Industrial State. Remember all those utopias in which the human from *now* says to the being of *then,* "You don't seem to be envious or jealous," and the being replies, "Oh, we've done away with envy and jealousy"? The being never tells the human how they did it. Well, we presumably will get over our problems and live in a world made to the specifications of academic snobs *because* we will achieve the Post Industrial State, and we will have achieved the Post Industrial State when we live as our new Greeks would have hoi polloi live. Alas, *even* if machines produce everything and plan it all for us (note the persistence of that fine old Puritan distinction between work and living), we shall still have to be highly interdependent and even time conscious just to take it away. There is not a single argument propounded by our best Futurists that promises to flatten out our curves toward limits except by simple assertion that the Post Industrial State will have changed all that.

Modernization as we know the process is something quite new under the sun. Early on in this book that newness was hung on the characteristics of modernization as a sort of universal social solvent. After all, even the invention of the wheel did not spread so virulently. The last previous universal solvents of "human" actions were presumably those brain or other mutations that produced homo sapiens —and in doing so perhaps doomed other protohuman species. The only comparable features prior to the development of modernization in the history of humankind were presumably changes that we still would analyze in terms of the biological evolution of the species. There is, however, another respect in which modernization is new. Many of the individual traits of the modernized, which have been mentioned above, can trace authentic pedigrees very far into our past. There have been instances before of education for an unknown future; there have been people who went in and out of contact with strangers, even casually; there have been many of the other features mentioned. Never before, however, did any considerable set of peoples put all of these traits together as a highly interdependent whole and expect them to touch, not small minorities of their populations, but virtually everyone. To make these characteristics into a set with a special Gestalt and to generalize that set ideally and/or actually to a vast majority of the populations concerned—that's new.

I have stressed above the things that seem to me most curious and queer, given the long stretch of humankind's experience. One of the queerest things of all is that we take this unusual combination of characteristics so very much for granted. It is fashionable for people my age to deplore the lack of knowledge of history among the young, but one of the characteristics of the modernized, whether young or old, is a lack of knowledge about the history of that very phenomenon, modernization. In the history of the world what we consider to be modernized is still very young, indeed. I do not consider modernization in the sense discussed here to be present anywhere, however modestly developed, until some time into the nineteenth century. If you make the phenomenon of modernization coterminous with the Industrial Revolution, you add no more than a century or so to that life history. I think that almost no one would consider highly modernized societies to have existed for more than a century, and many would consider such levels of development of the phenomenon to postdate World War I, or maybe even World War II. If you consider human generations to occur at thirty-year intervals, the phenomenon has encompassed fewer than two or no more than five depending on which starting point you pick. If you set the generation difference at fifteen years, it is under four or no more than ten. We have had history for something in excess of 5,000 years, and archaeologists and physical anthropologists, presumably, know something of how long before that human beings and their societies existed.

Many allegations made earlier in this work are about the characteristics of all nonmodernized societies that seem to have existed with various ups and downs in human contexts for thousands, if not hundreds of thousands, of years. They may have taken radically different forms, but they certainly lasted in one form or another for some thousands of years. The set of characteristics of the modernized societies taken together has existed for only a blip on the human time scale. Practically every prediction of our future has in common one whopper of an assumption—that we and our descendents have a future. I think it is highly questionable whether this set of characteristics taken together will be viable for humankind.

The demographers tell us that the problem of population densities alone will lick us if we continue to depart much from zero rates of population growth over any extended set of centuries. In this they are buttressed by all sorts of psychological and physiological studies, which tell us of the dyscrasias of other species when their members become "crowded." On each and every one of the subjects treated above, there is a real question whether or not human beings can adjust over any extended period of time to situations of this sort. There are surely dimensions of each and every one of these problems beyond which adjustments cannot take place. For example, how far can one carry education for an unknown future? Professor Margaret Mead has called attention to what she refers to as the prefigurative culture, by which she seems to mean that the freedom of the affluent young may make it possible for them to hit on ideas with which they can teach their elders. The young may, as a matter of course, do prodigies on the computer that only experts among the middle-aged can achieve, but that does not begin to strike at the heart of this problem. There is absolutely no a priori reason to believe that any amount of freedom to cast about in that fashion will result in either the young or the old hitting on means for educating the young for an unknown future. This is especially true since casting about with many degrees of freedom (and those are always easier to exaggerate than they are to establish) and high moral tone never guarantees that one will hit on rational findings—or even relevant ones. The young may learn to educate us in particulars without either they or us learning to educate themselves or us in general.

There is no question that there is an upper limit on the rapidity of social change to which human beings can adjust. We don't know what that upper limit is, but we have never even tried to cope with rates of change of the type we've already encountered. So far we've gone quite far in adjusting to fleeting casual contacts with strangers, but on all sides the old and the young alike cry out against loneliness and separation. Whole schools of psychology and sociology base the therapy that passes as their analysis on the warm moist heap theory of human preferences. They may very well be right. The organizational contexts to which we adjust constitute another problem—a twofold problem. First, there is the question of how many organizations one can adjust to, and we have already carried that beyond anyone's wildest imagination in earlier history. The second question is, of course, whether substantial numbers of people can adjust over very long periods of time to all of these highly specialized contexts. Like fleeting casual contacts with strangers, we seem to have gone quite far in this direction already. The kind of relationships that we emphasize to a much higher degree than have ever before been emphasized by others in history have a built-in kind of instability about them, since the longer they last in any given instance, the greater is the probability that they turn into some form of the kind of relationship that we allege gets in the way of being efficient and modern.

What are the factors that compensate? Do any? The high levels of affluence are easy to see in some quarters, though we are by no means sure that they can be generalized to the population of the planet as a whole. My guess is that they can be, and without undue pollution, but that, as a minimum, it is going to take levels of thinking and levels of execution that are not presently present. One thing is absolutely certain about such dispensations: they cannot take place at all without levels of regimentation [1] hitherto undreamt.

---

[1] Call them coordination or even communalization, if you prefer. Seek them by force, or love, or true belief, but do not expect them from great increases in tolerant rationality or great increases in tolerant rationality from them.

There are interesting special adjustments that depend on human orientation to materialism. Perhaps the outstanding one of these is the *trickle effect*. For the trickle effect to work, the following four conditions must obtain: (1) there are people highly motivated to seek social mobility; (2) there are high levels of snobbery; (3) there is a constant flow of new types of goods and services, preferably expensive ones, that are first introduced to those of higher income (and remember that's going to be highly correlated with high prestige); and (4) simultaneously there is also sufficiently even distribution of income so that others lower down in the income scale can hope to acquire those goods and services after they have achieved a certain prestigeful association. When these four conditions obtain, the constant trickle of those goods and services down through the various levels of prestige gives even those who are in fact highly stationary the feeling that they are ascending the greasy pole of social mobility. It's much the same sort of impression that one gets when one's train is standing still in Pennsylvania Station and the train on the opposite side of the platform pulls out in the opposite direction. As their train starts for Boston, you feel your train has started on its way to Princeton, late though it is.

For the trickle effect to operate, however, other things must continue to hold. There must be snobbery; there must be some unevenness of income distribution; and there must be a high sustained interest in material factors that many are likely to interpret as greed.

Suffice it to say that there are an extraordinary number of factors associated with modernization about which the very recency of our experience might lead us to be chary. We can trace out a clear possibility, if not probability, of increasing levels of frustration for every one of these. Increasingly on all sides, all of our movies, all of our television shows, all of our newspapers, all of our university students and faculties, and so forth make us well aware of what Pareto referred to as the need of demonstrating sentiments by overt acts. On all sides, using all sorts of philosophical cover, practically everyone seems to agree that violence follows such increases of stress and strain as the night follows the day. People agree on that whether they decry the violence or glorify it. At high governmental levels we are particularly alarmed about the prospects of such violence because the tools for the expression of violence at the disposal of any sorts of units capable of large-scale capital formation have reached a level of destructiveness that impresses us all. Even if a fairy godmother were to guarantee us absolutely against a mass holocaust in the name of any given state or states, we should by no means be out of the woods as far as survival is concerned, for individual reactions to these pressures, either of violence or of apathy, will make impossible those increasingly delicate interstitial adjustments of the closely concatenated processes of modernized society. The death rate associated with a world reformed in the image of our new consciousness would be as great or greater than the death rate in a world conforming to the image of our hawks. Modernized people, because of the delicacy of their interstitial adjustments, are highly vulnerable either to not giving a damn or to giving the wrong damn—and we're not even sure what the right damn is.

There are at least two other types of problems that pose special questions for our future: problems of the sex ratio and of centralization. First, let's have a try at centralization again. It's the easiest one to envisage doing something about. While we may not like its solution with increases of regimentation and lowering of freedoms and all of the rest, it is conceivable that there may be a purely cognitive solution to such questions. Rather, it would be more accurate to put it as follows. If we are to keep it going in some sense and continue life along with it, there are, simply, two elements to problems of centralization. One element is that of motivating people to go along with the increasing levels of coordination and control. Here the clear-cut limitation is that you can never do it by coercion alone, no matter how much you may worship strong arms. As a minimum, any worshipper of coercion is always defeated by the age-old question of "who guards the guards themselves." The one thing we know for sure is that we can never attain levels of centralization solely by coercive means. On the other hand, just in the spirit of analyzing a problem as it were, that needn't be a major concern for us. However unpretty it may be, the history of the world has been filled with people who seem to have adjusted rather easily by our standards to extremely high levels of restrictions on their freedom of behavior. This may have been a result of the fact that their horizons of the possible have been extremely limited, and we can't keep those limited in the face of high levels of modernization. In any case, however, it is possible to be sanguine—if that's the word for it—about the possibility of getting individuals to adjust to high levels of centralization.

Even if we get people to adjust well to that, even if they like it—and there's lots of hope for that in the fact that in all human history there have been many more sheep than Judas goats or other leaders—there would still be that second element, the terrible cognitive problem already mentioned above about centralization. The more highly centralized a system becomes, the greater is the probability that any error made by anyone or any set of ones setting orders or quotas or the like will spread catastrophically, or beneficently if that should be the implication of the error, to all parts of the system. It is sufficient for pessimism to realize that regardless of how many beneficent errors there may be, there is sooner or later bound to be at least one that has far-reaching catastrophic implications.

The greatest threat to viability posed by increasing levels of centralization is not, alas, the menace to human freedom but the increased probability of the stupidity death. In the presence of knowledge, the avoidance of catastrophic error is a function of motivation. In the presence of ignorance, it is a function of luck. What is at stake here is not any new knowledge of morals or anything of that sort—no new form of consciousness. Whatever the acceptable range of moral values may be, there will remain the strict engineering questions of whether one line of procedure as opposed to another will approximate those results. We do not begin to have adequate knowledge from the social sciences or any alternative source. You are as free and as qualified as I to speculate on whether we are likely to acquire such knowledge in time.

We may or may not learn to handle our sexual revolution already mentioned (See Chapter 10), but there is another sexual revolution that is about to break upon us (see above pp. 39–40). Humankind appears to be on the verge of being able to decide the sex of offspring at conception at will. As indicated above, when that is possible, if the means are cheap and readily acceptable on other grounds, two other uniformities about human conduct will come into play. The first is that the vast majority of all males have expressed an overwhelming preference for male offspring. The second is that so have the vast majority of all females. With such a technological breakthrough, the sex ratio of roughly one to one will change in the direction of several males to each female, say, ten to one. One may speculate indefinitely on whether or not the law of supply and demand is likely to operate in this connection. It is not likely to operate in the ordinary way or in time. The people who will be inconvenienced by the imbalance in sex ratio by contrast with what has previously existed will not be the parents having the children. For the most relevant cohorts, their own corrective action cannot possibly help themselves—even assuming they wish to do so. Furthermore, here again male vanity to the contrary notwithstanding, it is not the number of males that is crucial from many points of view. It is the number of females. It is the number of females, above all, that will determine the possibilities of further reproduction. If the preference for males stops at a two to one ratio, the ladies will still have to wish or be forced to wish at least 50 percent more children in order to replace themselves. If the ratio is much higher, their appetites will have to be, or be forced, higher. If neither their preferences for males nor their appetite for numbers of children change, the result will be a decline in population. Over the long run with such a new technology, in the absence of such changes, we would become extinct. Controlled fertility may turn out to be as disastrous for human survival as careless willful fertility. Having extinguished so many, we might achieve a species first in extinguishing ourselves by our sex preferences—the ultimate in male chauvinism. No doubt frenzied televised appeals and suitable economic inducements can offset all this—if they can be agreed upon in time.

This line of radical change with possibly nonviable implications for modernized societies is one that we may be able to offset. It might be difficult to effectuate means of offsetting it, but it is not difficult to visualize them. There is a closely related possibility, however, that is more serious although it would take more time for full effect. There has been speculation that the ratio of male to female fetuses at conception is very much higher than the ratio of male to female infants at birth. It is suspected that a considerable proportion of early miscarriages represent miscarriages of male fetuses. As indicated above (p. 37), the male is estimated by some to be less viable *in utero,* as he is in later life. It may very well be that at least 50 percent of those miscarriages, or more, may be miscarriages as a result of lethal genes, but there seems to be a respectable body of biological opinion that holds that many such miscarriages may be the result of correctable ph balances in the womb, and the like. Many of these miscarriages may be the result of factors that can be corrected with no dangers beyond the normal of perpetuating monsters. If that proves to be correct, if we find therapies for handling these dyscrasias, and if the male to female ratio at conception is in fact considerably higher than at birth, that ratio will come to be considerably higher at birth than it is at present. It might jump to say 115:100 or perhaps even to 125:100. Such a change as that will take much longer to bring about a population decline, let alone the most radical general social changes in history, than the technological advance previously mentioned, but it will be just as certain to do so over time and even more difficult to stop. It may not be possible to stop the implications of that one without selected male abortions or a male-oriented *mabiki*—a male infanticide. So it may go.

The question of whether we can survive is an interesting one. Most of the speculation about it today is conducted in terms of whether we can predict that the things we do today will make ecological continuance impossible. This may be a very long-range optimistic view of the question. Even where we know what we must do to survive, we may lack the will to do it or the ability to get together with others who have the same will. We may lack those for one of two general types of reasons. It may be inconsistent with the nature of human beings—physiological, psychological, and/or social—that we have that will. There may be in this sense physical or biological limitations on our having that will. Most of us will regard that possibility as premature biological pessimism, if not an unforgivable sort of determinism. On the other hand, it may be that the stresses and strains of modernization are such that none of us is likely to have that will—or an insufficient number of us is likely to have that will—even if we have the relevant knowledge. Either way, we may pass.

But what are we likely to become if the patterns of modernization are viable ones for humankind? The biggest implication of this possibility is more of the same already sketched above. If the above traits of modernization obtain and are viable, none of them taken singly or together seems to contain the seeds of self-deceleration. I do not even see any possibility of their rates of acceleration flattening out, although here we may say with some certainty that if these patterns are viable, the rates of acceleration of these processes cannot continue ever upward, and the curves themselves must flatten out as they approach some limit.

More concretely, two lines of speculation have some basis in the analysis that led here. The first has to do with highly modernized peoples; the second has to do with non-modernized ones. The highly modernized ones will see increasing convergence among them. As some theoretically complete state of modernization is approached, for whoever achieve it, the Russians and the Americans, the English and the Germans, the Japanese and the Chinese, the Africans and the Latins—all of us—will come to have increasingly more in common with one another than we have distinct from one another. More and more of what all peoples do will be explicable in terms of the phenomena of modernization, and less and less will be explicable in terms of the historical bases from which these departures took place. In the past all that humankind had in common was largely explicable in terms of qualities they shared as human beings. For the highly modernized all they have in common will increasingly be explicable in terms of the qualities they share as modernized human beings. That will only be a restrictive subset of the characteristics previously possible for humans in general.

The future with regard to latecomers to the process is by no means necessarily one of convergence, unless they become highly modernized. So far the number of societies whose peoples have become highly modernized is so restricted, and the experience apart from that of cases like Japan so feckless with regard to this process, that one of the possible projections may be continual fluctuation in the limbo of modernization—never able to return fully to the indigenous patterns before the new influences made themselves felt and never able to become highly modernized either. However interesting the phenomena may be, it is not likely to be pleasant for those involved.

One final word. You will note that I have made no references in this essay to any of the ideological clichés in terms of which these subjects are generally discussed. I have not talked of the special characteristics of capitalism or communism or socialism or fascism. The distinction between first, second, and third worlds for all their appeals to the senses have not been invoked as independent variables at any point along the line. I have not done so for a very simple reason. I think the matters discussed above as variables and constants are the most generally significant ones as far as this process of modernization is concerned. As far as my personal values are concerned, I would welcome being proved wrong about any one of these points. If the above factors are the critical patterns of this process in some sense, then one further thing is clear. Not a single one of them varies as a dependent variable of the ideological clichés in terms of which these matters are generally discussed. Education for an unknown future, fleeting casual contacts with strangers, rapid rates of change, high levels of centralization, shifts in the curve of income distribution, the forms of education, exotic organizational contexts, the domination and supervision of children on the way to maturity, the relations between rural and urban settings, increased uses of money—not a single solitary one of these varies as a dependent function of whether one is speaking about communists or capitalists or socialists or fascists or the world of the flower children or the New Left or the Nazis or any of the great political ideologies in terms of which we coin clichés. If the matters treated here are important, and if they are important at the most general levels of consideration of these problems, then the ideological clichés, which deter most of us most of the time, are not relevant. They are more than a waste of time; they are a set of blinders. I would not say that this is a "Look, Ma, no ideology" approach, since at least one definition of ideology makes an ideology of anything that establishes a point of view—and there is certainly a point of view here. I do hold that our current ideological clichés and formulae contain no answers and pose few if any of the right questions.

Index

abortions, male, 146
academic snobbery, 48–49*n.*, 92, 104, 136
actual and ideal patterns of human behavior, 33–41
affluence, 41, 82, 103, 108–109, 135, 139, 140
African freedom chanters, 110
age distinction, 112–114
aged, education and re-education of, 46; family as form of social insurance for, 129–130; value placed on, 128–129
agriculture, 18, 94–96
Albania, 6
alienation, matrifocality and, 118
American farm program, idiocy of, 95
anthropologists, 57, 138
anthropology, 27
apathy, 142
archaeologists, 138
Aristotle, 118*n.*
armed forces, higher education and, 104–105; modernization and, 74–80
Army Corps of Engineers, United States, 78
arson, 111

asceticism, 10; of poverty, 89; of striving for mastery over the things of this world, 89; of true belief, 89
assets, lack of direct convertibility of, 16–19
Australia, 7
authoritarianism, centralization and, 74
autonomy, individual and subgroup, 73*n.*
avoidance, emphases on, 76, 122–124

"bad" centralization, 23, 67–68. *See also* decentralization
barren marriages, 128
basic common curriculum, sharing of, 100
basic education, 51, 99–100, 103, 105, 106
bigotry, 11, 136
biological evolution of the species, 137
biological pessimism, premature, 147
birth control, 39
bottle feeding, 115*n.*
Brahmins, 90*n.*
breast feeding, 115*n.*

Index

conspicuous modernization, 16
consumer goods, heavy: mass acquisition of, 88
contacts with strangers, 56–59, 61–63, 123, 137, 139–140, 149
cooperative organizations, 50
coordination, 140n.
coordination and control, 15–16, 21–25, 69; military forces and, 75, 79; motivation and, 143
creativity, interference with, 66
cross-cousin marriage systems, 38n.
crowded, affluent . . . , 135
cultural diffusions, 5

damn, not giving a, 142
David, 34
day-care centers, 25
decentralization, 21, 23–24, 65, 67–69, 82; decision-making and, 73–74n.; in local and state governance, 68–69; population densities and, 131
decision-making, 3n.; decentralization and, 73–74n.
demographic changes, 127–131
demographic explosion, 39, 67, 72, 128, 131
demographic subsistence, 38, 127
demography, 27; utility of, 127
despotism, 21, 65

direct aid, 17
direct convertibility of assets, lack of, 16–19
Douglas-Lincoln debates, 110n.

ecological continuance, possibility of, 72, 146–147
ecological problems, 21, 55, 72, 88–89
economic determinism, 10
economic growth, 19–21
economic organizations, 60–61
economics, 27
economic sciences, 74n.
educational organizations (see schools)
educational systems, 14–15
education, of the aged, 46; basic, 51, 99–100, 103, 105, 106; co-, 116; family contexts and, 24–25, 43, 47–48, 50–51, 62, 101–102, 112, 115, 116; higher (see higher education); for a known future, 50–51, 65–66; for modernization, 99–107; secondary, 103; social contexts and, 50; specialized, 48, 62, 99–100, 106; in terms of schools, 24, 48, 62, 98, 101–102; tutelage, 101; universal, 98–100; for an unknown future, 42–51, 53, 55, 98, 118, 137, 139, 149
egalitarianism, 70–71, 122
elite colleges, 104

Index

heavy consumer goods, mass acquisition of, 88
hierarchical relationships, 122–123
hierarchy, acceptance of, 70, 71
higher education, 103–107; academic snobbery and, 48–49n., 104; armed forces contexts, 104–105; in China, 85; governance and, 104; in Japan, 103; money value and, 83; widespread, tendency toward, 103–104
historical literacy, 27
Hobbes, Thomas, 90n.
home-away-from-home, 53
horizons of the possible, 9
human behavior, ideal and actual patterns of, 33–41
humanism, lack of, 136
human life, sentimentality about preservation of, 130
husbandry, 18
hypocrisy, virtuosity in, 36

ideal and actual patterns of human behavior, 33–41
ideological clichés, 11, 148 149
idiocy of American farm program, 95
ignorance death, 72
Imperial China, 125n.
imperialism, 8, 14, 32
impersonal recruitment, emphases on, 122–126
income distribution, 21, 41,

84–92, 149; in China, 85; in India, 88; in Japan, 92; power and, 83, 87, 89–91; prestige and, 89–92, 141; in Soviet Union, 91, 92; in United States, 86–88, 91–92
incompetence, promotion to level of, 105
indebtedness, foreign: perils of, 17
India, Brahmins of, 90n.; income distribution, 88; religious fighting, 110
individual autonomy, 73n.
industrialization, 23, 95; conspicuous, 16
Industrial Revolution, 138
infanticide, male, 146
infant mortality rates, 128
inflation, 19
intellectual snobs, 34
interdependency, 12, 17, 18, 25, 44–45, 66–67, 69, 72, 73–74n.; population density and, 89, 131
internal maintenance of law and order, armed forces and, 74, 75
international trade, 17
Israel, 7; nonmilitary use of armed forces, 77
Iyeyasu, Tokugawa, 94

Japan, 6–7, 14, 148; "demos" of, 110; economic growth, 20; higher education, 103; income distribution, 92; literacy rates, 15, 99; New Left, 92; transformation and, 23

155

Index

sex of offspring, control of, 39–40, 144–145
sex ratios, imbalance in, 144–146; among modernized people, 128; among polygynous peoples, 37–38; in rural and urban centers, 119
sexual revolution, 112–120, 144
sexual segregation, 115–116
Shakespeare, William, 118n.
slavery, 34
snobbery, 141; academic, 48–49n., 104, 136; intellectual, 34
social change (see change)
social conquests, 5
social contexts, education and, 50
social heredity, 76
socialism, 11, 148, 149
social mobility, 96–97, 141
social planning, 15, 71–73; of income distribution, 91
social sciences, 27, 31, 32, 35, 72, 144
social scientists, 57, 135
sociologists, 57, 135
sociology, 27, 112
solitary, poor . . . , 135
South Africa, 7
South America, 7
South Korea, 95
Soviet Union, 6, 26; income distribution, 91, 92
Spain, 6
specialized learning, 48, 62, 99–100, 106
specialized organizations, 60–64. See also schools

species, biological evolution of, 137
state governance, decentralization in, 68, 69n.
Stengel, Casey, 129
store of value, money as, 83
strangers, contacts with, 56–59, 61–63, 123, 137, 139–140, 149
stress, violence and, 142
stupidity death, 72, 73, 144
subgroup autonomy, 73n.
subsistence, demographic, 38, 127; margin of, 87, 96, 129
suburban homes, 53

Taiwan, 95
taxes, 93–94; levying and collection of, 69n.; negative income, 86–87
technical knowledge, moral knowledge and, 73
technological change, 44–45, 52, 136–137, 146
television, 20, 44, 53, 110, 141–142
third-worldism, 11, 12, 148
three-car family, 53
Tokyo, strangers in, 57–58
towns and villages, relationship between, 93–97
tradition, modernization and, 121
traffic, centralization of, 67
transformation, 23
transmission of knowledge, 105, 106
trickle effect, 141
true belief, asceticism of, 89
tutors, 101
two-car family, 53

United States, 6, 12, 14, 26;
academic snobbery in, 48–
49*n.*, 104; care of the aged,
128; economic aid to Latin
America, 27; farm pro-
gram, idiocy of, 95; gross
national product per capita,
19, 20; income distribution,
86–88, 91–92; inflation, 19;
military-industrial complex,
78; nonmilitary use of armed
forces, 74–75, 78–79; po-
litical participation in, 109–
110; population problem,
67; productivity, 19, 20, 95;
public works projects, 78;
as repository of world university resources, 106; slavery, 34
United States Army Corps of
Engineers, 78
universal car ownership, 53
universal conscription, 75,
79*n.*, 105
universal education, 98–100
universal literacy, 14, 99
universal social solvent, modernization as, 3–11, 45,
136–137
universities, contributions of,
105–107. *See also* higher
education
university campuses, political
participation on, 110
unknown future, education
for, 42–51, 53, 55, 98, 118
137, 139, 149

urban centers, highly modernized, 7; population shifts to,
119; and rural centers, relationship between, 93–97;
sex ratios in, 119
urban homes, 53
usury, 93–94

value, money and, 73*n.*, 82–
83
Van de Walle, E., 115*n.*
Veblen, Thorstein, 12, 16, 23,
66
Venetian city-states, 93
Vietnam, 21–22, 95
village organizations, 50
villages and towns, relationship between, 93–97
violence, matrifocality and,
118; radical change and,
54, 118–120; recreational
exhilaration in, 110–111;
sexual revolution and, 119–
120; stress and, 142

war, 41, 52, 116
war games of brinkmanship,
72
wealth, 41
Weber, Max, 4, 89
Westoff, C., 39–40
wheel, invention of, 136–137
Woodstock affair, 110
working and living, distinction
between, 108, 136
world income, redistribution
of, 88